PUBLISHED

Jane Austen: *Emma*   DAVID LODGE
Jane Austen: *'Northanger Abbey' & 'Persuasion'*   B.C. SOU⌐
Jane Austen: *'Sense and Sensibility'*, *'Pride and Prejudic⌐*
   Park'   P.C. SOUTHAM
William Blake: *Songs of Innoce⌐ and Experien⌐*   MARGAR⌐ ⌐LL
Charlotte Brontë: *'Jane Eyre' & 'Villette'*   MIRIAM ALLOTT
Emily Brontë: *Wuthering Heights*   MIRIAM ALLOTT
Browning: *'Men and Women' & Other Poems*   J.R. WATSON
Bunyan: *The Pilgrim's Progress*   ROGER SHARROCK
Chaucer: *Canterbury Tales*   J.J. ANDERSON
Coleridge: *'The Ancient Mariner' & Other Poems*   ALUN R. JONES & WILLIAM
   TYDEMAN
Congreve: *Comedies*   PATRICK LYONS
Conrad: *'Heart of Darkness', 'Nostromo' & 'Under Western Eyes'*   C.B. COX
Conrad: *The Secret Agent*   IAN WATT
Dickens: *Bleak House*   A.E. DYSON
Dickens: *'Hard Times', 'Great Expectations' & 'Our Mutual Friend'*   NORMAN
   PAGE
Dickens: *'Dombey and Son' & 'Little Dorrit'*   ALAN SHELSTON
Donne: *Songs and Sonets*   JULIAN LOVELOCK
George Eliot: *Middlemarch*   PATRICK SWINDEN
George Eliot: *'The Mill on the Floss' & 'Silas Marner'*   R.P. DRAPER
T.S. Eliot: *Four Quartets*   BERNARD BERGONZI
T.S. Eliot: *'Prufrock', 'Gerontion', 'Ash Wednesday' & Other Shorter Poems*
   B.C. SOUTHAM
T.S. Eliot: *The Waste Land*   C.B. COX & ARNOLD P. HINCHLIFFE
T.S. Eliot: *Plays*   ARNOLD P. HINCHLIFFE
Henry Fielding: *Tom Jones*   NEIL COMPTON
E.M. Forster: *A Passage to India*   MALCOLM BRADBURY
William Golding: *Novels 1954-64*   NORMAN PAGE
Hardy: *The Tragic Novels*   R.P. DRAPER
Hardy: *Poems*   JAMES GIBSON & TREVOR JOHNSON
Gerard Manley Hopkins: MARGARET BOTTRALL
Henry James: *'Washington Square' & 'The Portrait of a Lady'*   ALAN SHELSTON
Jonson: *Volpone*   JONAS A. BARISH
Jonson: *'Every Man in his Humour' & 'The Alchemist'*   R.V. HOLDSWORTH
James Joyce: *'Dubliners' & 'A Portrait of the Artist as a Young Man'*   MORRIS
   BEJA
Keats: *Odes*   G.S. FRASER
Keats: *Narrative Poems*   JOHN SPENCER HILL
D.H. Lawrence: *Sons and Lovers*   GAMINI SALGADO
D.H. Lawrence: *'The Rainbow' & 'Women in Love'*   COLIN CLARKE
Marlowe: *Doctor Faustus*   JOHN JUMP
Marlowe: *'Tamburlaine the Great', 'Edward the Second' & 'The Jew of*
   Malta'   JOHN RUSSELL BROWN
Marvell: *Poems*   ARTHUR POLLARD
Milton: *Paradise Lost*   A.E. DYSON & JULIAN LOVELOCK
O'Casey: *'Juno and the Paycock', 'The Plough and the Stars' & 'The Shadow of a*
   Gunman'   RONALD AYLING
John Osborne: *Look Back in Anger*   JOHN RUSSELL TAYLOR

OTHER CASEBOOKS ARE IN PREPARATION

John Osborne
Look Back in Anger

A CASEBOOK

EDITED BY

JOHN RUSSELL TAYLOR

**MACMILLAN
EDUCATION**

Selection and editorial matter
© John Russell Taylor 1968

First published 1968
6th reprint 1987

Published by
MACMILLAN EDUCATION LTD
Houndmills, Basingstoke, Hampshire
RG21 2XS
and London
Companies and representatives
throughout the world

Printed in Hong Kong

ISBN 0–333–08400–4

CONTENTS

Part 4: *Some Foreign Reviews*

Part 5: *Points of View*

ACKNOWLEDGEMENTS

REVIEWS of the first performance in *The Times, News Chronicle, Daily Mail, Financial Times, The Guardian, The Star. Evening Standard, Daily Telegraph, Evening News, Daily Worker, Sunday Express, Birmingham Post, Daily Sketch, Daily Express, Daily Mirror, Sunday Times, Observer, New Statesman, Spectator* and *Punch* (The Editors); John Osborne, 'The Epistle to the Philistines', from *Tribune*, 13 May 1960, 'That Awful Museum', from *Twentieth Century*, February 1961 (Twentieth Century Magazine Ltd), 'A Letter to My Fellow Countrymen', from *Tribune*, 18 August 1961, and 'On Critics and Criticism', from the *Sunday Telegraph*, 28 August 1966 (David Higham Associates Ltd); John Russell Taylor, *Anger and After* (Methuen & Co. Ltd, Hill & Wang Inc.) and *'Inadmissible Evidence'* (Encore Publishing Co. Ltd); Katharine J. Worth, 'The Angry Young Man', from *Experimental Drama* (G. Bell & Sons Ltd); George E. Wellwarth, *Theatre of Paradox and Protest* (MacGibbon & Kee Ltd, New York University Press); Geoffrey Carnall, 'Saints and Human Beings: Orwell, Osborne and Gandhi' (first published by Rajasthan University Press); Edwin Morgan, 'That Uncertain Feeling' (Encore Publishing Co. Ltd); John Mander, *The Writer and Commitment* (Secker & Warburg Ltd); Mary McCarthy, *Sights and Spectacles* (William Heinemann Ltd, Farrar, Straus & Giroux Inc.); Charles Marowitz, 'The Ascension of John Osborne', from the *Tulane Drama Review*, VII (Winter 1962) ii (© *Tulane Drama Review* 1962); John Gassner, *Theatre at the Crossroads* (Holt, Rinehart & Winston Inc.; © Mollie Gassner 1960); Allardyce Nicoll, 'Somewhat in a New Dimension', from *Contemporary Theatre* (Edward Arnold (Publishers) Ltd); Laurence Kitchin, *Mid-Century Drama* (Faber & Faber Ltd); James Gindin, *Postwar British Fiction*

(University of California Press); 'An Osborne Symposium', from a National Theatre programme (The National Theatre, Alan Sillitoe, Peter Brook, Angus Wilson, John Arden, Tony Richardson and George Steiner); Lindsay Anderson, 'Stand Up, Stand Up!' from *Sight and Sound*, Autumn 1956; Stuart Hall, 'Something to Live For', and extracts by Tom Milne and Arthur Miller (Encore Publishing Co. Ltd); Harold Clurman, *Lies Like Truth* (The Macmillan Company).

In a few cases the publishers have been unable to trace the copyright-owners, but they will be happy to make the necessary arrangements at the first opportunity.

GENERAL EDITOR'S PREFACE

EACH of this series of Casebooks concerns either one well-known and influential work of literature or two or three closely linked works. The main section consists of critical readings, mostly modern, brought together from journals and books. A selection of reviews and comments by the author's contemporaries is also included, and sometimes comments from the author himself. The Editor's Introduction charts the reputation of the work from its first appearance until the present time.

What is the purpose of such a collection? Chiefly, to assist reading. Our first response to literature may be, or seem to be, 'personal'. Certain qualities of vigour, profundity, beauty or 'truth to experience' strike us, and the work gains a foothold in our mind. Later, an isolated phrase or passage may return to haunt or illuminate. Where did we hear that? we wonder – it could scarcely be better put.

In these and similar ways appreciation begins, but major literature prompts to very much more. There are certain facts we need to know if we are to understand properly. Who were the author's original readers, and what assumptions did he share with them? What was his theory of literature? Was he committed to a particular historical situation, or to a set of beliefs? We need historians as well as critics to help us with this. But there are also more purely literary factors to take account of: the work's structure and rhetoric; its symbols and archetypes; its tone, genre and texture; its use of language; the words on the page. In all these matters critics can inform and enrich our individual responses by offering imaginative recreations of their own.

For the life of a book is not, after all, merely 'personal'; it is more like a tripartite dialogue, between a writer living 'then', a reader living 'now', and whatever forces of survival and honour link the two. Criticism is the public manifestation of this dialogue, a witness to the continuing power of literature to arouse and excite. It illuminates the possibilities and rewards of the dialogue, pushing 'interpretation' as far forward as it can go.

And here, indeed, is the rub: how far can it go? Where does 'interpretation' end and nonsense begin? Why is one interpretation superior to another, and why does each age need to interpret for itself? The critic knows that his insights have value only in so far as they serve the text, and that he must take account of views differing sharply from his own. He knows that his own writing will be judged as well as the work he writes about, so that he cannot simply assert inner illumination or a differing taste.

The critical forum is a place of vigorous conflict and disagreement, but there is nothing in this to cause dismay. What is attested is the complexity of human experience and the richness of literature, not any chaos or relativity of taste. A critic is better seen, no doubt, as an explorer than as an 'authority', but explorers ought to be, and usually are, well equipped. The effect of good criticism is to convince us of what C. S. Lewis called 'the enormous extension of our being which we owe to authors'. A Casebook will be justified only if it helps to promote the same end.

A single volume can represent no more than a small selection of critical opinions. Some critics have been excluded for reasons of space, and it is hoped that readers will follow up the further suggestions in the Select Bibliography. Other contributions have been severed from their original context, to which some readers may wish to return. Indeed, if they take a hint from the critics represented here, they certainly will.

A. E. DYSON

INTRODUCTION

THERE is little difficulty in judging the lasting interest and appeal
of a literary work which has survived and continued to be read
two or three hundred years after its first appearance: it is very
much a matter of Q.E.D. With anything written within the last
fifty, or even more the last twenty, years we are in a very different
critical situation. It would be a bold man indeed who felt
inclined to pontificate on which plays of our own day will still
be performed, which poems and novels still read, in a century's
time, let alone at what level they will stand in critical estimation.
Will Osborne be the mid-twentieth-century equivalent of
Marlowe, say – read and studied and even from time to time
successfully reintroduced into the living theatrical repertory? Or
might he be an Otway, exciting a certain amount of scholarly
interest and respect which tend to remain all the same of a
decidedly academic cast? Or will he, like James Sheridan Knowles,
be no more than a name in the history books? It is impossible
to say. And also, from our point of view today, irrelevant.

For John Osborne and *Look Back in Anger* are interesting
to us now as much for what they stand for as for what they are.
It is not still too early to hope that we may reach some sort of
critical conclusions about them, but we can hardly expect that
those conclusions will be of lasting validity. On the other hand,
Look Back in Anger, wherever it may ultimately stand in
twentieth-century British drama, or even in the final accounting
of John Osborne's own work, has its unarguable importance as
the beginning of a revolution in the British theatre, and as the
central and most immediately influential expression of the mood
of its time, the mood of the 'angry young man'.

Though the whole movement of thought and feeling summed

up in the phrase 'angry young man' is so relatively recent, it already has a quaint period ring to it. Understandably, considering that by 1970 more than half Britain's population will be under 25, that is, born after the Second World War, too young to remember the first post-war Labour Government, and the very oldest of them just about readying themselves for the 11-plus at the time of Suez and the Hungarian Revolution. No past is so imaginatively remote as such recent past, just out of one's own field of vision and not yet far enough away to be history. *Look Back in Anger* is a key to this period, but in order to know how to use it – and perhaps to want to use it – we must look at the outside events which brought about, in a number of young and not quite so young writers of the time, the frame of mind it embodies.

Much of the emotional history of the period between the end of the war and *Look Back in Anger* (1956) is suggested in Lindsay Anderson's essay 'Stand Up! Stand Up!' Those who, actually or metaphorically, celebrated the Labour Party's victory in the 1945 elections by 'nailing a red flag to the roof of the mess at the foot of Annan Parbat' believed that they were signalling the start of a new era. In the past was India, the raj, the imperial tradition; ahead was a Socialist utopia. But, of course, realities hardly ever live up to visions. The Labour Government proved as apt to compromise as any other sort of government; and even where it did not, where it introduced a whole system of social security and all that goes to make up the Welfare State, young idealists were still left feeling that there must be something more. All should be right with the world, and yet somehow it wasn't. In 1951 we had the Festival of Britain to celebrate our new artistic and technological achievements, and in the midst of it all the Labour Government, returned with a precariously small majority a year or so before, was defeated at the polls and the Conservatives were back. So much for the social revolution; and it did not even improve matters very much in the eyes of the young and idealistic that the new Government accepted its fruits and did not, as had confidently been predicted, immediately set about dismantling the Welfare State.

In fact, the two major parties in Britain seemed to be gradually moving together. And whatever the practical advantages of this situation, it had the result of disillusioning many who had formerly been active in politics and believed that political activity held the solution for the world's ills. What, after all, was the point of politics if in the end it did not seem to make any noticeable difference which party one voted for? Consequently the dissatisfaction which many people felt with life in the early 1950s became curiously aimless. There was no obvious focus for resentment on the political scene, or for that matter any real hope to set against present dissatisfactions: no longer was it open to any moderately realistic person to suppose that everything would be different if only one party were out of power and the other in. Or so, at any rate, it seemed to many intelligent young men and women in those years. They were in precisely the situation that Jimmy Porter outlines in one of the most famous speeches from *Look Back in Anger*, when he says,

I suppose people of our generation aren't able to die for good causes any longer. We had all that done for us, in the 'thirties and 'forties, when we were still kids. There aren't any good, brave causes left.

Clearly, something was brewing. So much unlocalised, unorganised resentment must find expression in some way. And, as so often happens, the first signs of its expression were literary. To be precise, there were two forms of expression, both in literature and, after a brief time lag, in life. They might be capsulated as cynicism and rededication. The cynical line is approximately that taken by the authors of two popular and influential novels of the time, Kingsley Amis's *Lucky Jim* (1954) and John Wain's *Hurry on Down* (1953). The heroes of these are shamelessly self-centred, liberated from social responsibility, out for number one. They are sexy, ill-mannered and bent on cocking a snook at social conventions and class limitations. Thus they can, with a bit of forcing, be regarded as rebels, defiers of the *status quo*, irreverent outsiders sniping at the existing structure of British society. But if they are all these things, it is with no deliberate intent, no serious programme: they have just decided, as individuals, to contract out of whatever in modern British life does not happen to suit them. If there are indeed no good causes left, they are cheerfully reconciled to a life without causes.

On the other side of the coin was rededication. To the cry that there are no causes left it might always be answered that we think this because we are pampered and anaesthetised to the sufferings of others. What we need to do is to look around, see what there is to protest about, and then dedicate ourselves to protesting in whatever way seems most effective – it will probably not be a directly party-political way. As it happened, 1956, the year of *Look Back in Anger*, was rather rich in causes for agitation – or disillusionment, depending which way one chose to look at it. In Hungary the people rebelled against their Russian-imposed Communist Government, and Russia put down the revolt in a good old-fashioned imperialist way by sending in tanks, while the rest of the world looked on and did nothing. In the Mediterranean the Egyptian Government announced that it was taking over the Suez Canal, up to then owned and run by Anglo-French interests. In a surprising attempt to revive nineteenth-century gunboat-diplomacy, Britain and France sent in troops to protect their interests in the Suez area. The result was that after taking over the Canal Zone they found themselves virtually without support in the world, and had to hand their conquest over to the United Nations, who then handed it back to Egypt. The whole adventure proved nothing except that the days for such would-be grand imperial gestures were over and that Britain must accept a back seat in the conduct of the world. Meanwhile at home 'protest' was organising itself round the question of nuclear disarmament. Directly political action was avoided: instead individuals got together in non-party groups to offer passive resistance of various sorts ('sitting down' in the streets was much favoured) and particularly to march to Aldermaston, an airbase where nuclear weapons were kept.

All these happenings contributed to the climate of opinion in which *Look Back in Anger* first appeared and gradually built itself into a success. The particular advantage it had in doing this was the character of its hero, Jimmy Porter. By a happy accident, no doubt, his attitudes were strategically situated between those of the cynics and those of the 'committed' idealists. Like so many of the heroes of the *Lucky Jim* type of novel, he is socially adrift, in rebellion, or at least reaction, against the social and educational system which has helped to shape him, and determined, whatever he does, not to act in the way 'they' might expect him to. On the other hand, though his picture of the situation of Britain is very much that of the cynical heroes, and though his sexual opportunism and his boorishness or impatience with social niceties would seem to ally him with them, his bitterness and anguish carry him further over in the direction of the self-organising protesters: if he can find no cause to fight for, he nevertheless speaks eloquently of the need for such a cause, the necessity of the search for one.

Jimmy Porter was thus ideally constituted to be the all-purpose hero of the dissatisfied young. But of course to achieve this position he had not only to speak, but also, most importantly, to be heard. And in May 1956 the theatre would have seemed a rather unlikely place for this to occur. Nobody doubted that the British theatre had been in precipitate decline since the end of the war. Audiences had been falling off and theatres closing all over the country – a process accelerated rapidly by the starting-up of television after a wartime break. Moreover, creatively British drama had been stagnating. The most successful dramatist in Britain at this time was Terence Rattigan, a conscientious and intelligent craftsman who specialised in solid emotional dramas with good meaty acting roles. But then his first success, *French Without Tears*, dated right back to 1936, so he could hardly be regarded as a rising young talent. The main cause for excitement in the post-war London theatre had been the unexpected box-office success of a series of verse-plays by Christopher Fry, which, along with a couple of plays by the senior T. S. Eliot and a scattering of other theatrical ventures by established poets, were held to constitute a revival of poetic drama. Fry's light, whimsical verse-fantasies are at the moment so far out of fashion it is almost impossible to attempt a balanced estimate of them.

But it is certain that the particular sort of escapism they offered was less and less what the theatre-going public required, and it is perhaps significant that after *Look Back in Anger*, and all that its success ushered in, this previously very prolific dramatist produced only one stage play in twelve years.

In the theatre the time is always ripe for an exciting new talent. But in 1956 it was even riper than usual. A new group, the English Stage Company, had been set up at the Royal Court Theatre, somewhat off the normal West End theatrical map, with the declared intention of becoming a writers' theatre. Many other companies had begun in the same spirit, with the same high ideals, and succumbed all too rapidly to the commercial pressures of London theatre. The English Stage Company might easily have gone the same way if it had not been for *Look Back in Anger*, which just came to them through the post in answer to an advertisement for new drama. Its author, a 26-year-old actor of no particular distinction, had not had any play previously produced in London and had no literary reputation whatever. The English Stage Company liked the play and decided to put it on as their first by a new author, in repertory with plays by Arthur Miller, the established novelist Angus Wilson, and the well-known verse-dramatist Ronald Duncan.

It was to prove a happy decision. Though the play got a good deal of critical attention on its opening, of which more in a moment, it did not immediately establish itself as a hit. It did well enough to justify its being kept on for a short run on its own after the first repertory season ended, but it continued to play at a little below break-even figures until something rather interesting happened. The Company agreed to let an Act of it be shown on television (something normally done only when a play is doing so well nothing can harm it or so badly that nothing can come to it but good). And at once the takings leapt up, nearly doubling in two weeks. Clearly the play, by being seen in part on television, by television's mass audience, had managed to leap the gap generally filled, if at all, by the theatre critics. Audiences used to going to the theatre did not have, in this instance, to rely entirely on what the critics said in order to decide if they should go to the play or not: they were given a sample and were able to judge directly for themselves. Moreover, other people, who were probably not regular theatregoers, were presented in their own homes with a bit of this play. If they liked it, if it spoke to them, they might be moved to see the whole thing for themselves. The 'new drama' which followed on the success of *Look Back in Anger* has clearly found a new audience, or a number of different new audiences. *Look Back in Anger* was only the first to demonstrate that television, feared rival of the theatre, might provide a valuable means of finding new theatre-goers, untrammelled by traditional ideas of what did and did not constitute a good evening in the theatre.

It should not be understood from this, though, that *Look Back in Anger* succeeded largely in spite of the critics. Though in recent years the legend has grown up that when it opened it was greeted with almost universal incomprehension and dislike until Kenneth Tynan in the *Observer* saved the day with a glowing recommendation, this is in fact far from being the case. Tynan was certainly the most unequivocally enthusiastic, but the reception of the play, or at any rate of the playwright, was almost uniformly favourable. With a couple of exceptions everyone agreed that Mr Osborne was a dramatist to watch and that this was just the sort of thing required to justify the new company's existence.

T. C. Worsley in the *New Statesman*, for example, caught the prevailing opinion very well when he wrote: 'As a play *Look Back in Anger* hardly exists. The author has written all the soliloquies for his Wolverhampton Hamlet and virtually left out all the other characters and all the action. But in these soliloquies you can hear the authentic new tone of the Nineteen-Fifties, desperate, savage, resentful and, at times, very funny. This is the kind of play which, for all its imperfections, the English Stage Company ought to be doing. . . .' In the *Daily Express* John Barber put the same view rather more briskly: 'It is intense, angry, feverish, undisciplined. It is even crazy. But it is young, young, young.' In the *Financial Times* Derek Granger, describing *Look Back in Anger* as 'this arresting, painful and sometimes

astonishing first play', said of it: 'Mr Osborne communicates no
sense to us that he has taken even three paces back from the work
that has so hotly and tormentedly engaged him. But for all that
this is a play of extraordinary importance. Certainly it seems to
have given the English Stage Company its first really excited
sense of occasion. And its influence should go far beyond such
an eccentric and contorted one-man turn as the controversial
Waiting for Godot.'

Even those who had more serious doubts about the play itself
found Osborne an exciting new writer. Cecil Wilson in the
Daily Mail felt that the English Stage Company 'have not
discovered a masterpiece, but they *have* discovered a dramatist
of outstanding promise: a man who can write with a searing
passion, but happens in this case to have lavished it on the wrong
play. . . . The repetitiousness cries out for the knife. But through
all the author's overwriting and laborious shock tactics, we can
perceive what a brilliant play this young man will write when he
has got this one out of his system and let a little sunshine into
his soul.' The *Daily Worker* agreed, remarking that the play
'starts rich in promise, but lets us down with a sickening
melodramatic thud', and concluding that Osborne's 'development as a writer will depend on what he looks forward to'.
For Milton Shulman in the *Evening Standard, Look Back in
Anger* 'aims at being a despairing cry, but achieves only the
stature of a self-pitying snivel. . . . But underneath the rasping,
negative whine of this play one can distinguish the considerable
promise of its author. Mr John Osborne has a dazzling aptitude
for provoking and stimulating dialogue, and he draws character
with firm convincing strokes. When he stops being angry – or
when he lets us in on what he is angry about – he may write a
very good play.'

Of the three 'quality' dailies the *Manchester Guardian* (as it
then was) and the *Daily Telegraph* were, on the whole, more for
than against. Philip Hope-Wallace called it 'this strongly felt
but rather muddled first drama', and concluded that 'It is by
no means a total success artistically, but it has enough tension,
feeling and originality of theme to make the [English Stage

Company's] choice understandable. . . . I believe that they have got a potential playwright at last. . . .' In the *Telegraph* Patrick Gibbs thought it 'a work of some power, uncertainly directed'. Only *The Times* came out decidedly against ('This first play has passages of good violent writing, but its total gesture is altogether inadequate'), in which opinion it found support only in the *Daily Mirror* ('An angry play by an angry young author . . . neurotic, exaggerated and more than slightly distasteful') and the *Birmingham Post* ('We shall be very frank about this. If more plays like tonight's *Look Back in Anger* are produced, the "Writers' Theatre" at the Royal Court must surely sink. I look back with anger upon a night misconceived and mis-spent.').

Then came Sunday, with a generally favourable review from Harold Hobson in the *Sunday Times* and Kenneth Tynan's great outburst of enthusiasm in the *Observer* which ended: 'I agree that *Look Back in Anger* is likely to remain a minority taste. What matters, however, is the size of the minority. I estimate it at roughly 6,733,000, which is the number of people in this country between twenty and thirty. . . . I doubt if I could love anyone who did not wish to see *Look Back in Anger*. It is the best young play of its decade.'

The general accent of the first critical reaction, obviously, was on the novelty of what Osborne was saying and on the sort of character he chose for his hero. As might be expected, later and more considered critical attention has gone rather to the making of connections between Osborne's attitudes and those of earlier writers, and to the examination of precisely what technical means he uses in *Look Back in Anger* to put those attitudes over. If Jimmy Porter still seems to be the extreme embodiment of a particular state of mind, and therefore a key figure in the study of a period when that state of mind was the most influential in intellectual and artistic circles, it was inevitable that further consideration should reveal earlier writers for whom in general the answer to life was likewise 'no'. An obvious parallel might be found among those writers who threw all their energies into the Spanish Civil War during the latter 1930s and then, when Franco won and the whole thing proved to be only a dress rehearsal for a full-scale fight against fascism in the 1940s, became disorientated and disillusioned and mostly wandered off to find more comfortable private solutions to the problems of life in the United States. But a favoured stalking-horse for Osborne has been someone who, though involved in the Spanish Civil War, was quite outside this particular circle: George Orwell, whose hatred of the present, fear of the future and disdain mixed with potent nostalgia for the past suggest an obvious relationship with Osborne.

As for the technical side of *Look Back in Anger*, Osborne himself has been in the forefront of the revaluers: by 1961 he was ready to describe it as 'a formal, rather old-fashioned play'. And immediately after *Look Back in Anger* he had already begun to break away from the traditional naturalism of the play's surface-style by making use in his next play, *The Entertainer*, of non-realistic devices derived from the practice of Brecht. In *Look Back in Anger*, it now appears, he was using a structure handed on to him from the most conventional theatrical craftsmen of his apprenticeship. It was only the force (disruptive as far as this structure was concerned) of Jimmy Porter's rhetoric which distinguished *Look Back in Anger* from such traditional pieces as Rattigan's *The Deep Blue Sea*. Clearly in *Look Back in Anger* something is happening to the everyday language of the British theatre normal at that time; but the changes are still potential and partial. Despite what the critic of the *Financial Times* said about the play in relation to *Waiting for Godot*, the fact remains (it was realised by few more quickly than Osborne himself) that a play like *Look Back in Anger* seems technically anachronistic after *Waiting for Godot*. It is anyway significant that influential though Osborne's success was in persuading managers to try out other young writers in the theatre, *Look Back in Anger* had surprisingly little influence on either the subject-matter or the style of the dramatists who came after – of Harold Pinter, John Arden, N. F. Simpson, Ann Jellicoe, Arnold Wesker, Henry Livings, to name only a few of the more important.

Finally, there is the inescapable question of where the play stands in critical estimation now. The easiest and most obvious answer is that it doesn't. Coherent critical revaluation tends to be contingent on some obvious occasion. Such an occasion might be provided if, for instance – it is not entirely impossible – the National Theatre were to put on a full-dress revival. That would force the critics to think again, to come to terms with their immediate reactions to the play in the late 1960s instead of the mid 1950s, instead of inclining to refer back mentally to the way it all seemed then and presume, as it is human nature to do, that those first reactions remain valid. If one may generalise meanwhile in the absence of very much concrete evidence, it seems that those coming to the play for the first time now, or somehow finding themselves constrained to read it afresh or watch an amateur revival, on the whole find both its good and its bad qualities intensified. Jimmy's rhetoric is still as forceful as ever, and he remains, however dislikable, at least genuinely magnetic. On the other hand the feebleness of the opposition presented to him, the relatively shadowy characterisation of those around him, is more evident now than ever it was, and not only the bears-and-squirrels game but a lot concerned with the character of Alison's father seems positively sentimental.

On the other hand, it is only fair to say that *Look Back in Anger* remains just the effective beginning of a career which has continued to develop during the years between; it is Osborne's first word, and not by a long way his last. Moreover, of all the dramatists who have been thrown up by Britain's theatrical New Wave, Osborne alone has succeeded, whatever anyone may say against his work, in getting through to a mass public, in achieving a broadness and amplitude of utterance which have carried him far beyond the clubs and coteries. That is already a lot. Just how much only the passage of another forty years or so will enable us to decide for sure.

JOHN RUSSELL TAYLOR

GENERAL EDITOR'S COMMENTS

'WHERE does the play stand in critical estimation now?' This question must fascinate anyone who remembers the electric tension of the Royal Court in 1956. No evening in the theatre since has seemed quite as stirring. How far was this due to the political fever of that extraordinary year – Hungary, Suez, the campaign against capital punishment, the rise of C.N.D. – and how far to the actual merits of the play? It was a time of anger certainly, and of the particular anger of the young. The young were making their first concerted bid for ascendancy, and it was in 1956 or thereabouts that swinging Britain, as we have learned to call it, began.

No wonder that *Look Back in Anger* turned into myth within weeks of its opening, and passed into universal currency for political debate. By 1958, an angry young man was anyone from a teddy-boy to a young don at Redbrick, from a teenaged pop singer having his fifth breakdown to Lord Altrincham (then the aristocratic scourge of monarchy: now, democratically, Mr John Grigg).

The myth ensured the play's success, but also its distortion; it passed into history, or pseudo-history, too soon. A student of mine recently suggested that it should be revived in modern dress. Precisely: but what modern dress? Last year's beads and bells are history too, and way back beyond the leather jackets and the mod gear, the jeans and T shirts, the polo-neck sweaters, what have Jimmy Porter's 'worn tweed jacket and flannels' to do with us? Where now is his anger? The present young were six or seven years old when he ranted, and not worrying about Suez overmuch. They grew up to their ascendancy, Mary Quant and the Beatles, O.B.E.s and hippies, with the Ad. men and fashion designers, the T.V. men and Sunday colour-photographers in control, to turn them from anger ao more profitable things. The young change their image or have it changed for them monthly: but Jimmy Porter's anger *was* real and spontaneous, and typical in 1956 of an articulate minority, at any rate, of the young.

This is one reason why the play will survive, I believe, its own hectic period, and take its place among the major works of the theatre in our time. It is a genuine drama, about real events and people, and was not designed for the *kind* of success which it actually had. I am still willing to risk the critical estimate which I formulated in 1959, that it is a major play – and this despite the fact that I haven't seen it produced recently, and cannot visualise quite how, at this present moment, it should be 'done'. The period problems loom large, for the reasons the editor discusses, but in the future they will recede again, inevitably, into place. Meanwhile, *Look Back in Anger* seems to me not a crudely propagandist play, as has sometimes been asserted, but a valid study of a highly complex personality at odds with his world. Certain enigmas, touching both the hero himself and the validity of his anger, are central to the effect. Jimmy Porter is not only a warm-hearted idealist raging against the evils of man and the universe, he is also a cruel and even morbid misfit in a group of reasonably normal and well-disposed people. This paradox in his status is inescapable, and the serious concern with the nature of evil, and of anger, which makes the play absorbing depends upon our continuing awareness of it. During the action, we witness a number of characters acting, interacting, discussing one another critically, making and retracting choices – and this in the setting of certain important symbols (the bears and squirrels, the church bells, the ironing-board, the trumpet and so on) which impose dramatic coherence, though not moral finality, on what happens. The construction is taut, and theatrically exciting; the ideas are stimulating, and the final effect is not of any kind of certainty – there is no *genre* direction, for instance – but of realistic, and challenging, enigma. As for Jimmy himself, one cannot doubt that a character so troubled and complex should owe something to his creator, any more than one would doubt that Shakespeare found the possibilities of Hamlet in himself, and Ibsen of Halvard Solness. But, as with these other instances, it is impossible to imagine that the creator is identified with his creation, or even committed to approval untinged by irony and doubt. Such characters are placed in dramatic situations in which their potentialities for insight and creativity are balanced, and often overwhelmed, by interrelated capacities for destructive illusion: the dramatic context, no less than the central character, embodies the experience of the play. (*Hamlet*, if one likes to put it this way, could not possibly have been written by Hamlet.)

In *Look Back in Anger*, the setting and action reflect searching irony on the hero, of a kind which forces us to see that even if John Osborne intended elements of self-portrait then he did so in no uncritical mood (the comparison with Gregers Werle, Ibsen's savagely ironic self-portrait in *The Wild Duck*, may seem apt). Again, if Jimmy is offered as a 'typical' hero, he is so as Hamlet is – a recognisable and recurring type, and perhaps also a permanent possibility in the make-up of any sensitive person, but in a minority in any generation, and in most individuals resolutely suppressed.

How, then, have the myth and the oversimplified interpretation distorted him? Partly through the author's undoubted concern for the contemporary scene, and the extreme authenticity of his depiction of Jimmy's world. To the many insights about this witnessed by this Casebook not much can be added, though my own stress would fall very much on the hydrogen bomb. Though the Bomb is mentioned only twice, one feels throughout its effect upon the moral imagination of a generation, in the limits which it sets both to personal heroism and to 'the future', as incentives to hope and action. Remembering the type of participation in Spain which seemed possible to intellectuals of Jimmy's type in 1937, and the inevitable paralysis imposed on their counterparts at the time of Hungary nineteen years later, one can feel that the play is as subtly aware of the psychological impact of the Bomb on men of Jimmy's temperament as anything else in recent literature. Again, consider the place of 'the Establishment' in the play. Protests against insensitivity and

hypocrisy in Church and State have been more or less constant
features of Western civilisation, at least since those of Christ
himself, and Jimmy's main complaints are little different in
content from those of (say) D. H. Lawrence thirty years before.
But the tone is different, and distinctive. It belongs to a generation which comes after the Second World War, after the Attlee
administration, and is becoming aware in this new situation of
several things: the totally false euphoria of the 'New Elizabethan
Age'; the perennial success of the middle classes against those
who try to take their own ideals too seriously; and again, the
Bomb – that factor, new to the world since the death of Lawrence,
whose effects upon humanity have still to be fully understood.
One's final feeling is that one is hearing the age-old voice of
moral outrage, but hearing it authentically in the post-atomic
age.

When this is allowed, a critic returns to the character of
Jimmy, who expresses, but is not contained by, such truths.
Obviously, he is not an ideal character. He suffers, is frustrated,
and makes terribly wrong choices – as the last scene makes clear,
even for those who imagine that his blasphemy against life when
he hopes that Alison 'will have a baby, and that it will die' is a
mere expression of John Osborne's sense of values. The case
against him is not one that can be made with any suspicion that
one is catching John Osborne out: clues of the most explicit kind
are provided in the first stage direction:

Jimmy is a tall, thin young man about twenty-five, wearing a
very worn tweed jacket and flannels. . . . He is a disconcerting
mixture of sincerity and cheerful malice, of tenderness and freebooting cruelty; restless, importunate, full of pride, a combination which alienates the sensitive and insensitive alike. Blistering honesty, or apparent honesty, like his, makes few friends. To
many he may seem sensitive to the point of vulgarity. To others,
he is simply a loudmouth. To be as vehement as he is is to be
almost non-committal.

The doubts suggested here by 'or apparent honesty', 'to the
point of vulgarity', 'almost non-committal' are sufficiently
striking, and from Jimmy's first appearance his anger is no less

ambiguous than himself. It is a commonplace of morality to
point out that anger can be anything from an indispensable virtue
to a most dangerous vice, and that between these extremes every
shade of reality and illusion, nobility and bitterness, can often
be detected. Notoriously, it is a chameleon emotion, changing
colour and mood unnoticed, and subtly allowing the best in a
man to offer sanctions to the worst. A moralist might offer specific
reflections on this, as, for example, that anger is good when it is
selfless, compassionate, and allied to positive action; evil when it is
selfish, or tainted with frustration, malice, and the desire to
destroy. A creative artist depicting the emotion is more likely
to be alive to ways in which most anger hovers between these
two poles in most actual men and situations; and *Look Back in
Anger* is a moral exploration in precisely this field. In Jimmy
Porter, one is confronted with a man whose anger undoubtedly
starts in human idealism, and the desire that men should be more
honest, more alive, more human than they normally are. Very
soon, however, corruption creeps in. Jimmy's sense of outrage
is so little controlled by either selflessness, stoicism or any clear
discipline of the mind that it readily degenerates into moods
profoundly destructive to life. The alarming juxtapositions in
his make-up, with a holy crusade against stupidity on the one
side, and a neurotic shrinking from in-laws and church bells on
the other, cannot be escaped. His motives are hopelessly mixed.
One can never be sure whether his anger with Alison centres in a
genuine desire to save her, or in an ugly type of possessiveness
heavily disguised. His targets are inconsistent. He lashes at Cliff
both for not reading the *New Statesman* and for reading it; he
taunts his wife with her education and Cliff with his ignorance.
From the start, it is clear that, rightly or wrongly, he has not
acquired the normal techniques for accepting suffering, and that
he regards his morbid sensitivity to it as evidence of moral
superiority. He becomes convinced that he is the only one who
really *knows* what suffering is, and that he has the right to scourge
those less agitated than himself. There are marked symptoms
of a persecution complex, both in the tenacity with which he
clings to his working-class origin as an occasion for masochism,

and in his readiness to see his wife's continued correspondence with her parents in terms of conspiracy and betrayal. His tenderness for his wife (the real tenderness implied in the bears-and-squirrels game as well as elsewhere) is unable to dispel the restless suspicions which turn love into conquest, marriage into revenge, and the normal reticences of others into insult. More sinister than this, he has the iconoclasm peculiar to that most dangerous type, the frustrated messiah, who because he cannot save the world comes to feel the desire to destroy it instead. Much of the time, his deeds and imagery are deliberately calculated to shock. In attempting to hurt his wife, he outrages every decency of love and of life itself, the certainty of his moral mission to her merely justifying every savagery of tone and mood he can command. All of this goes, as one might expect, with a peculiar sensitivity to shock on his own part. He can accept neither life nor death with ease. The sound of church bells torments him with the thought of possible worlds other than his own.

The result in practice is that his ideals suffer shipwreck along with himself. Though his impieties are often safely and admirably based, the pieties that should sustain them – whether to God, or Man, or Nature as they *might* be beyond the mazes of human error – are seldom in view. His genuine affection for Cliff and love for Alison are at the mercy of his anger rather than directing it as they should. His trumpet can mock the universe but not sound a call to battle; he becomes an emotional liability to those whom he seeks to inspire.

In all this, Osborne's concern is to offer the truth of a situation, not to offer final moral reflections on what it means. As I have suggested, those who imagine that doubts about Jimmy's character somehow escaped the attention of his creator must have a very naïve view of how plays come to be written. On the other hand, those who imagine that the case against Jimmy is all that the play offers overlook certain other data at least as clear. It is significant that Alison and Cliff, and later even Helena, feel that Jimmy is basically worth while. They may not accept his ideas – and Alison at one stage decides that her sanity depends upon getting away from him – but they never doubt that his torment is at root that of a good man, and that he deserves success, whether he has the secret of finding it or not. Also, they sense that his anger has in it elements of honesty and courage that might be redemptive if they could ever be released into effective action. Helena thinks that he is born out of his time, and should have lived in the days of the French Revolution. Alison's image of him is always that of a knight in armour. In matters of personal morality, he stands opposed to Pharisees and Laodiceans alike. He is on the side of engagement, whatever else might be said.

Much is revealed through his relationship with the two women in the play – who seem to me sufficiently characterised, even though one would have liked more roundness and depth. First, Helena, since she is easy to deal with: an entirely honest character, from a world poles apart from Jimmy's own. She is middle-class not only by birth, but by instinct and conviction; which is why she is essentially disruptive to Jimmy, both when she conspires against him, and when she seduces him (to his great surprise). This, also, is why she can never really hurt him as Alison can. She interferes with his marriage for Alison's good, since she honestly thinks (and this need not even be rationalisation) that Alison will be better out of the 'madhouse'; and she takes Jimmy for herself because she finds that she desires him, and wants to have him for a time. At no stage, however, does she allow her values to be questioned by Jimmy, so that he can never think that she has come over into his camp, or be hurt by any sense of betrayal when she leaves. She believes all along that her affair is sinful, 'terribly wrong' as she tells Alison, and she knows that in the end Alison has 'all the rights'. Whereas Jimmy lives at war with the conventions, and believes that sincerity alone can govern human relationships, Helena is equally sure that the 'book of rules' is necessary to sanity, and says: 'At least, I still believe in right and wrong! Not even the months in this madhouse have stopped me doing that. Even though everything I have done is wrong, at least I have known it was wrong.' The affair between them has never touched her deeply, and the fact that her loyalty to conventions – whether through conviction, or fear, or even thoughtlessness scarcely matters – comes even before her loyalty to people makes this partly inevitable. Jimmy knows, presumably, that in this they are opposites, so that when she leaves him, making the break with characteristic toughness, he is resigned rather than angry, and hurt personally, but not at the level of his ideals.

Alison is far nearer to Jimmy, since he is trying to win not only her love, but her allegiance to his vision of life; a vision where the 'book of rules' must be closed at the outset, and committal worked out in individual terms. He comes to feel that Alison has betrayed him by coming over to him in marriage while remaining mentally and spiritually in the world of her parents. In a sense he is right, as her habits of thought when she leaves him, and even more when she discusses him with her father, make clear. She has responded to physical love, but not offered it; listened to ideals, but withheld enthusiasm; submitted to the attraction of Jimmy as a knight, but clung obstinately to the security of well-bred indifference in the face of his onslaughts. The most telling criticism of her attitude is made (interestingly) by her father, who says that like himself she enjoys sitting on the fence. She is surprised, and even hurt by this: 'I married him, didn't I?' is her immediate reply. But this middle-class defence clearly does not convince even her father, who sees as clearly as Jimmy himself that she has never given herself to her husband with the honesty which she knows he demands and needs.

The ending of the play is in these respects ambiguous. Jimmy, confronted with her real suffering and degradation, and the appalling knowledge that this is what, in his anger, he has been demanding of her, himself breaks under the strain and has to appeal for mercy. The confrontation seems to awaken him to the blasphemy, and immaturity, of his excesses of anger, and possibly purges it in that moment. Alison herself, having really suffered, and then come back, can be presumed to have realised her own defects, and to have returned with a deeper commitment to Jimmy's love. They revert to the bears-and-squirrels game, as a refuge from a world which sets 'cruel steel traps' for its animals. It seems possible that this basis of warm, animal love might, on the other side of suffering, lead to happiness, though some ritics think otherwise, and see in the ending only a temporary further escape into whimsy. Both possibilities are left open, and remarkably so in a play which has often been thought propagandist in aim.

Look Back in Anger also challenges us with Jimmy's unresolved quarrel with the universe. In one sense, the challenge is simple. Do we really think (and this is Jimmy's own formulation) that the voice raised in protest must always be a weakling's voice? Might it not sometimes be raised in authority, and with strength? Is failure to be at home in our present society merely adolescent maladjustment, or might it not be at least the beginning of grace? Is our awareness of sickness in Jimmy's anger all that requires to be noted, or is the major sickness in society, which reduces its potential knights to raging impotence? Osborne's honesty in exploring the ambiguities and weaknesses of anger is such that he allows escape, by way of such familiar routes as 'What are angry young men about?', 'Can't they take it like men?' to those who thrive in the *status quo*. But this escape is itself a form of trap, in that those who unreflectingly take it proclaim themselves moral cripples on the other side. To admire Jimmy Porter uncritically is to distort. Anyone with the least concern for human values, however, is bound to find in his anger not only evidences of immaturity, but also the type of conscience, and engagement, without which any supposed moral maturity is merely a sham.

Look Back in Anger is a play which increases understanding both of the morally tormented and of their torments. But it does more. It is a reminder of what rebel moralists are apt to be like, and of the strange mingling of sensitivity and cruelty, insight and wilfulness, idealism and cynicism which is not reserved for Jimmy Porter, or for his period, alone.

In a world which sometimes deals with its most challenging misfits by mocking or martyring them, and later venerating them for the wrong reasons, it is no bad thing to have a reminder like this. It is no bad thing, either, to be reminded of the closeness between the rhetoric of failure, and the rhetoric of success. My own impression is that *Look Back in Anger* offers permanent moral insights, and at least one splendid flesh-and-blood character. I cannot imagine actors at any future period being content to leave it on the shelf.

A. E. DYSON

PART ONE

Reviews of the First Performance, 8 May 1956

.

CAST LIST

Jimmy Porter	Kenneth Haigh
Cliff Lewis	Alan Bates
Alison Porter	Mary Ure
Helena Charles	Helena Hughes
Colonel Redfern	John Welsh

PRODUCED BY TONY RICHARDSON

THIS first play has passages of good violent writing, but its total gesture is altogether inadequate. A scruffy but eloquent hater of class distinctions is sadly deserted by his adoring wife. He makes do with her upper class friend for a while, but when his wife comes grovelling back the mistress magnanimously concludes that she has done wrong to break up the marriage. We are left in doubt whether this is a tribute to his powers as a lady killer or a victory for Bohemianism over stuffy respectability.

The piece consists largely of angry tirades. The hero regards himself, and clearly is regarded by the author, as the spokesman for the younger post-war generation which looks round at the world and finds nothing right with it. He shares his squalid Bohemia with his wife and a good-natured friend who helps him to run a sweet shop, and it is easy to understand that his restless disgruntlement, expressed in set speeches of great length and ferocity, must sooner or later make the place too uncomfortable for his companions. Much of his sharpest invective is directed against his wife's mother, who did not want her to marry into Bohemian squalor. The wife is the first to go, and the wonder is that she ever comes back. Mr Haigh contrives somehow to touch the aggressive talker with sympathy and to hint that he is the victim of some love–hate impulses that he cannot control. Mr Alan Bates is good as the long-suffering friend. Miss Helena Hughes gives neat theatrical effect to her sudden change from contempt to infatuation. And Miss Mary Ure suggests that the inarticulate wife really suffers. (*The Times*)

THIS is an interesting but less than successful offering by 26-year-old John Osborne. Jimmy Porter (Kenneth Haigh) is boorish and ultimately boring. His continuous tirade against life in the shabby flat he shares with his wife (Mary Ure) and a friend (Alan Bates) has a deadening effect upon the whole play – despite a fair leavening of good dialogue.

Directed by Tony Richardson, it is at least noteworthy for attempting to say *something* about contemporary life. (R. M.-T., in the *News Chronicle*)

JOHN OSBORNE is a 27-year-old actor who was out of work when he heard about this theatre's new repertory venture. He submitted his play out of the blue. The management not only accepted it but offered him small parts in their next two productions.

They have not discovered a masterpiece, but they *have* discovered a dramatist of outstanding promise: a man who can write with a searing passion, but happens in this case to have lavished it on the wrong play. Its essential wrongness lies in its leading character, a young neurotic full of intellectual frustration who lives like a pig and furiously finds the whole world out of step except himself.

His bitterness produces a fine flow of savage talk, but is basically a bore because its reasons are never clearly explained. His virtual monologue of self-pity and unrighteous indignation leaves one gasping for spiritual breath. The repetitiousness cries out for the knife. But, through all the author's overwriting and the laborious shock tactics, we can perceive what a brilliant play this young man will write when he has got this one out of his system and let a little sunshine into his soul.

Kenneth Haigh, a young actor who has impressed me before at the same theatre, lends a touch of early Olivier to a seething performance worthier of Hamlet than of this oaf. Mary Ure's beauty is frittered away on the part of a wife who, judging by the time she spends ironing, seems to have taken in the nation's laundry, and Helena Hughes and Alan Bates are left with little to do but look on aghast. (Cecil Wilson, in the *Daily Mail*)

THIS arresting, painful and sometimes astonishing first play by Mr John Osborne shows a small group of young people of the very present day living in a sorry state of emotional and physical squalor. In particular it throws up in a kind of arc-lit 'close-up' the marital relationship between an immensely resentful graduate of working-class origin and the passively resilient young woman he has snatched against all odds from a middle-class home.

The churlish note of the play's inception often grates; its characters – though they kick out like drunks in the arms of the police – frequently lack dramatic motivation (it is the business of theatre to be more convincing than life in this respect). Again, its terms are always shrill and sometimes affected. It deals with the most intimate aspects of close relationships in a way which might frigidly be described as inconsiderately passionate. As the effect is of raw experience immediately and unselectively transcribed it is almost as discomforting to watch at close quarters as the rows of one's friends.

Mr Osborne communicates no sense to us that he has taken even three paces back from the work that has so hotly and tormentedly engaged him. But for all this it is a play of extraordinary importance. Certainly it seems to have given the English Stage Company its first really excited sense of occasion. And its influence should go far, far beyond such an eccentric and contorted one-man turn as the controversial *Waiting for Godot*. The reasons for this are not far to seek. However one may object to the illogicality of much of Mr Osborne's detail in the matters of background painting, it is true that for the first time he has raised the curtain to show us those contemporary attitudes that so many of the post-war generation have adopted and in particular that 'raspberry-blowing' belligerency – it is the young's particularly prickly form of honesty – which is the result of a calm but absolute disillusionment. It is life, in fact, as many representatively dour and graceless young people now live it.

The strength, however, of Mr Osborne's writing is the very penetrating truth he displays in his treatment of his 'hero' and 'heroine'. It might be thought impossible that anyone so blatantly loutish as the former could survive as a central stage figure, let alone keep a wife for five years. He is mean, arrogant, self-pitying, cruelly abusive and so utterly disposed to feel injured that he hardly permits himself two consecutive moments of common civility. Yet we are quite persuaded that the passionate mutual rivalry of this ill-sorted marriage is in itself an unbreakable bond: and that it is in this ferocious domestic battle-course that mutual interdependence looms most large. The curious truth of this enables the play to survive much that is less convincing, and even the mildly ludicrous beginning to a third act where the husband changes partners with his wife's best friend.

Mr Kenneth Haigh [plays] the very unlucky Jim Porter whose life seems both such a mine-ridden shambles and such a desert of ennui. And he has enormously come to his author's aid in presenting us with a tiresome boorish oaf who is always – as intended – oddly sympathetic. Miss Mary Ure is a very touching figure when resigned to her sad little chores, but not quite convincing in moments of outbreak. There is also a vivid, realistic picture of a kindly oaf in gentle attendance as a lodger. Mr Tony Richardson has produced with what is doubtless the right brain-fagging metronomic rhythm of wet Sundays in the Midlands. But the household squalor is a little overdone and so is all that 'in the movement' trumpet playing. (Derek Granger, in the *Financial Times*)

THE English Stage Company for the third offering of its repertory season at the Royal Court Theatre last night brought forward a first play by a young man, John Osborne, called *Look Back in Anger*. It is by no means a total success artistically, but it has enough tension, feeling, and originality of theme and speech to make the choice understandable, and the evening must have given to anyone who has ever wrestled with the mechanics of play-making an uneasy and yet not wasted jaunt, just as it must have woken echoes in anyone who has not forgotten the frustrations of youth.

Mr Osborne's hero, a boor, a self-pitying, self-dramatising intellectual rebel who drives his wife away, takes a mistress and then drops her when, to his surprise, his wife comes crawling back, will not be thought an edifying example of chivalry. But those who have not lost the power to examine themselves will probably find something basically true in the prolix, shapeless study of a futile, frustrated wretch, even if they do not get as far as extending much sympathy to him. The brutish Polish husband of *A Streetcar Named Desire* was much less given to windy rhetoric: or at least he remained inarticulate. Tennessee Williams's characters exist and suffer rather than debate their frustration. But is the dilemma posed here in this ugly, cheerless Bohemia supposed to be typical?

The author and the actors too did not persuade us wholly that they really 'spoke for' a lost, maddened generation. There is the intention to be fair – even to the hated bourgeois parents of the cool and apparently unfeeling wife who is at length brought to heel by a miscarriage. The trouble seems to be in the overstatement of the hero's sense of grievance: like one of Strindberg's woman-haters, he ends in a kind of frenzied preaching in an empty conventicle. Neither we in the audience nor even the other Bohemians on the stage with him are really reacting to his anger. Numbness sets in.

Kenneth Haigh battled bravely with this awkward 'first-play' hero without being able to suggest much more than a spoilt and neurotic bore who badly needed the attention of an analyst. No sooner was sympathy quickened than it ebbed again. Mary Ure as the animal, patient wife, Helena Hughes as a friend who comes to stay and reign in the sordid attic, and Alan Bates as a cosy young puppy, that third party who sometimes holds a cracking marriage together, were more easily brought to life. Tony Richardson's production and a good set by Alan Tagg help out this strongly felt but rather muddled first drama. But I believe they have got a potential playwright at last, all the same. (Philip Hope-Wallace, in the *Manchester Guardian*)

THERE are enough clever lines in this first play by 27-year-old actor John Osborne to keep a more experienced playwright for life. For Mr Osborne pursues cleverness with a voracity equalled only by his youthful determination to shock us. He obviously wants to shake us into thinking that we are never quite clear what it is he wants us to think about. Is it the Class Struggle or simply sex? Both are inextricably mixed up in the mind of his hero, a caricature of the sort of frustrated left-wing intellectual who, I thought, died out during the war, and both are somewhat soiled. A bitter young misfit who can never forgive his pretty wife her middle-class origin, he pours out an endless flow of taunts and foul invective most of the evening and plays a trumpet in the bathroom during the remainder. 'I want to stand in your tears and splash about in them and sing. I want to see your face rubbed in the mud,' he says. This you will recognise, if you are acquainted with the modern realist school of writing, means 'I love you'.

In real life someone would surely have punched this self-pitying egotist on the nose and she would already have gone home to mother before the play starts. But that would have deprived Kenneth Haigh of the opportunity of impressing us with the assured way in which he puts over the long, savage tirades and with the feeling he still manages to bring to the play's rare tender moments. Mary Ure as his wife, Helena Hughes as her friend, and Alan Bates as a young Welshman contribute, mostly in effective silence, to the general atmosphere of bitterness and squalor into which is slipped with the reasonableness of reality some moments of crazy comedy.

In *Look Back in Anger*, Mr Osborne rakes a muckheap with the talent of an immature Tennessee Williams and wraps up his findings in a virtuoso display of passionate over-writing that makes us look forward in high hope to his next play. (Robert Wraight, in the *Star*)

NOTHING is so comforting to the young as the opportunity to feel sorry for themselves. Every generation automatically assumes that it has the exclusive, authentic, gilt-edged, divine right to be described as 'lost'. *Look Back in Anger* by John Osborne at the Royal Court Theatre sets up a wailing wall for the latest post-war generation of under-thirties. It aims at being a despairing cry but achieves only the stature of a self-pitying snivel.

In a one-room attic flat in the Midlands life for four young people is epitomised by a rainy Sunday afternoon squabbling about the Sunday papers, listening to concerts on noisy radios, contemplating a beer or the flicks, and the unending ironing of washing. In this cocoon of petty squalor and small thoughts most of them are content to hibernate. Theirs is a world of the aggressively young where it is good form to be outrageous and where ideas are loud rather than deep.

Fed up with their complacency and resignation is Jimmy Porter (Kenneth Haigh), who is constantly lashing himself into a frenzy about their smugness. 'Let's have a little game,' he shouts. 'Let's pretend we're human beings.' In a hurricane of ranting speeches he abuses his wife and his friends for having no beliefs, no convictions, no enthusiasms. But while he lashes out wildly in every direction, he never identifies the shadows he is attacking.

Indeed the failure of *Look Back in Anger* is its inability to be coherent about its despair. There is no real motivation behind Porter's bitterness. Why is a university-educated man running a sweet stall? What else does he want to do besides blow a trumpet? What has turned him into this pugnacious bore other than the fact that he saw his father die? We are left to work out our own causes. Futility is our only clue.

Contemptuously he dismisses religion, science, morality, or politics as having any acceptable solution to his problem. In a void of anger his only philosophy is the cynical guffaw. In the course of the play he loses his wife, his mistress and his best friend. And the audience too. But beneath the rasping, negative whine of this play one can distinguish the considerable promise of its author. Mr John Osborne has a dazzling aptitude for provoking and stimulating dialogue, and he draws characters with firm, convincing strokes. When he stops being angry – or when he lets us in on what he is angry about – he may write a very good play.

Mr Kenneth Haigh admirably catches the arrogance and doubt of a young man carrying a chip on his shoulder so large that it is knocking him off his mental balance. And Miss Mary Ure re-establishes her claim to be one of our most considerable young actresses with her touching and restrained performance as a wife who thought she married an idealist and found she had a paranoiac on her hands. (Milton Shulman, in the *Evening Standard*)

JOHN OSBORNE's *Look Back in Anger*, seen at the Royal Court last night, is the first play to be given by ,the English Stage Company from a new author. It is a work of some power, uncertainly directed.

The leading character, a man of education living in poverty, would seem to be intended as a full-length study in resentment. Something of a sadist and very much an exhibitionist, he has married above himself, apparently out of spite against middle-class respectability. His wife he lashes with a verbal fury that is often witty and always cruel. It is not, however, resentment that is personified as much as self-pity and this causes the sympathy, which the author intends, to be withdrawn. When his wife left him, it seemed she was fortunate. When she returned to him in the end, a broken spirit, were we intended to cheer?

A similar uncertainty was present throughout all the deliberations in the squalid attic flat – a nondescript man and a girl-friend of the wife's who becomes, briefly, the husband's mistress complete the audience for his passionate harangues on life and love. What the hero's predicament was, apart from the hint that he was 'born out of his time', I found difficult to decide. He was, perhaps, a character who should have gone to a psychiatrist rather than have come to a dramatist – not at any rate to one writing his first play. Kenneth Haigh acted this part with great vocal abandon, as if it had no problems, not getting much sympathy for the fellow but making much of his literary jokes. Mary Ure played the wife with a compelling simplicity. Tony

Richardson's production was forthright. (Patrick Gibbs, in the
Daily Telegraph)

YOUNG Jimmy Porter is furious with life. He addresses his nice
little wife, between spasms of rather rancid baby talk, in terms
one would hesitate to use to the lowest drab of the streets. He
bespatters his best friend with backwash from the jargon of
scruffy left-wing pseudo-intellectuals and then taunts him
because he is fortunate enough not to understand it. After four
years of marriage he hasn't yet wearied of fuming class-con-
sciously against his mother-in-law and gloating over the
indigestible feast the worms will have of her. He spits venom
against everything and everybody and is apparently convinced
that for the youth of today the world is an utterly putrid place.

This of course is the most putrid bosh, and I am dismayed to
learn that John Osborne, the 27-year-old author of *Look Back in
Anger*, sincerely believes his insufferable 'hero' to be representative of the younger generation. The trouble is not with the
world – which was never less putrid to people in their twenties –
but with a playwright who, having wit and an obvious turn for
forceful writing, wastes these gifts on a character who could
only be shaken into sense by being ducked in a horse pond or
sentenced to a lifetime of cleaning latrines. Yet the mere fact
that I look back in anger at Jimmy is proof that the author has an
unusual power to shock.

At the Royal Court Theatre, Kenneth Haigh plays this back-
street Hamlet with ingenious resource and variety. As a mere feat
of memory the performance is remarkable: for Jimmy, like all his
kind, is infatuated with the sound of his own voice. Mary Ure,
as the wife whose well-bred patience only stings him into
hysterical sadism, is also convincing, though one feels that any
girl of spirit would have walked out of this madhouse in three
weeks. Helena Hughes and Alan Bates tactfully dance attendance
on the egomaniac, but the play is really a *pas seul* for Jimmy.
(Stephen Williams, in the *Evening News*)

SUPERBLY acted by its cast of five, this play by 27-year-old actor-turned-author John Osborne starts rich in promise, but lets us down with a sickening melodramatic thud.

Conceived as a protest against the smug middle-class morality reflected in most conventional West End plays, it is set in a squalid one-roomed flat in a Midlands town – the kind of play Tennessee Williams might have written if he had spent a month of rainy Sundays in Birmingham. A young man, cynical, neurotic, of working-class stock, lashes his middle-class wife from one indignity to another. We laugh at some of his cynical jokes, but can feel no sympathy – not even pity – for a character who becomes almost as tiresome with his bitter pronouncements as the people he despises.

Mr Osborne's dialogue is fluent, often very funny (a chinless wonder from Sandhurst is described as 'a platitude from outer space'). He does indeed look back in anger. But his development as a writer will depend upon what he looks forward to. (P.G., in the *Daily Worker*)

WHAT Marlon Brando's script writers have done for the inarticulate American moron, Mr John Osborne has attempted to do in *Look Back in Anger* (Royal Court) for the over-articulate English phoney intellectual. This play is about Jimmy, a university chap of working-class background who lives in a filthy attic with his pretty wife whom he harangues continuously in horribly long, vicious, self-pitying speeches. He is looking back so angrily, apparently, because he watched his father die, hates his wife's middle-class parents, and can't think of anything constructive to think about. Jimmy is supposed to represent the post-war generation. In fact, he is simply a rather nasty type of pretentious bore.

Throughout the almost three hours of this funereally-produced piece Miss Mary Ure gives her best performance yet, as the pathetic little wife. Though I feel that this play is inept and banal, some people whose opinions I respect find it compelling and 'promising'. (Derek Monsey, in the *Sunday Express*)

WE should be very frank about this. If more plays like tonight's *Look Back in Anger* are produced, the 'Writers' Theatre' at the Royal Court must surely sink. I look back in anger upon a night misconceived and mis-spent. The author is a young actor called John Osborne. He is 27, and the claim is that 'as a representative of the younger generation he feels that he has every right to be very angry. Was any generation treated less fairly?'

This violent little play, set in a one-room flat in a large Midland town, does not establish one's belief in Mr Osborne as a mouthpiece of the younger generation. The principal character is self-pitying, uncouth, cheaply vulgar. I felt for most of the night that I was listening to an extension of some feebly rancid short story in a highly contemporary idiom. We are warned that the piece is controversial. I don't want to argue: I wonder only, in helpless distaste, whether this is a play to be done in a season that began with hope so eager.

Kenneth Haigh acts loyally in a part that seems to be a bitter monologue; and Mary Ure, Helena Hughes, and Alan Bates serve the author with care. But this is not the kind of evening to make us grateful to the English Stage Company. (J. C. Trewin, in the *Birmingham Post*)

JOHN OSBORNE is a 27-year-old actor, until recently un-employed, who believes his generation has been given a raw deal. So he has written a play on the subject. That it turned out last night the most exasperating play I've seen for years doesn't alter an important fact: Mr Osborne is a new dramatist of importance. He can create character, has a natural sense of drama and a ready turn of verbal wit.

From a dingy Midlands garret Mr Osborne's protagonist – a misfit with a dishful of chips on his shoulder – declaims against Life with literary flights of obscenity and cascades of self-pity. He reduces to a frenzy, fluently and by turn, his best friend, his wife and the girl who takes her place.

Kenneth Haigh acts, or bellows, the rôle to perfection – with occasional glimpses of tenderness. But it's Mary Ure, the insulted, quivering wife, disciplining her last remnants of spirit into

submissiveness, who gives the play its best quality. An exquisitely
moving performance which triumphs over indelicacies of dialogue, action and undress. (Harold Conway, in the *Daily Sketch*)

A FIRST play by an exciting new English writer – 27-year-old
John Osborne – burst on London last night. It is intense, angry,
feverish, undisciplined. It is even crazy. But it is young, young,
young. It is about a bitter man who has filched an upper-class
girl from her prim home. He pours out a vitriolic tirade against
the world. His wild and whirling words damn poverty, damn
tenderness, damn pity. His wife – a lovely, still Mary Ure –
listens in silence. Why is he so angry? He is young, frustrated,
unhappy. In fact, he is like thousands of young Londoners today.
His wife leaves him and he turns to her best friend. His wife
returns – and he finds that she has borne and lost a baby. She has
suffered: now she may understand him better.

Kenneth Haigh, in an extremely long role, is magnificent as
the impossible hero. 'Look, Ma, how unlike Terence Rattigan
I'm being,' was how Terence Rattigan summed up the new
playwright's approach. (John Barber, in the *Daily Express*)

AN angry play by an angry young author made its first appearance at the Royal Court Theatre last night. The trouble was that
Look Back in Anger was also neurotic, exaggerated and more
than slightly distasteful. But this English Stage Company
production drew a remarkable performance from Kenneth Haigh
as a youthful, loud-mouthed husband who would have been far
better off in a strait-jacket. He strode about a miserable one-room
attic flat belabouring his wife (Mary Ure) and everyone in sight
in a voice as incessant as a buzz-saw. He was a post-war failure.
Partly, according to the author, because he saw his father die and
partly because he ran a sweet stall.

John Osborne, twenty-seven-year-old actor, wrote the play.
It was accepted by the company when he was out of work. He
certainly poured a lot of bitterness into it. (Robert Tee, in the
Daily Mirror)

MR JOHN OSBORNE, the author of *Look Back in Anger*, is a writer who at present does not know what he is doing. He seems to think that he is crashing through the world with deadly right uppercuts, whereas all the time it is his unregarded left that is doing the damage. Though the blinkers still obscure his vision, he is a writer of outstanding promise, and the English Stage Company is to be congratulated on having discovered him.

There are really two plays in *Look Back in Anger*. One of them is ordinary and noisy, and Mr Osborne has written it with some wit but more prolixity; the other is sketched into the margin of the first, and consists of hardly any words at all, but is controlled by a fine and sympathetic imagination, and is superbly played, in long passages of pain and silence, by Miss Mary Ure. The play that, judging from the title of his work, and from the fact that one of the characters, Jimmy Porter, speaks more words than the rest of the company put together, Mr Osborne thinks he has written is yet another of youth's accusations against the world. Jimmy Porter is a young intellectual who, with his less bright-witted partner, Cliff Lewis, keeps a sweet-stall somewhere in the Midlands. He has been to a provincial university, has married Alison Redfern, a girl out of the upper middle classes, been despised and spied on by her relatives, lives in a squalid one-room flat, and reads, and comments on at enormous length, what he calls, in a sort of admiring hatred, the 'posh' Sunday papers.

His part is a long, sustained scream at society, literary critics, and his wife. Especially at his wife. She stands, for what seems whole days, at the ironing-board, smoothing trousers, shirts, ties, while he insults her in phrases of a passionate bitterness edged with a frustrated love. His complaints against her are endless; she has tried to keep some of her friends; she still clutches round her the rags of her old social smartness; she still writes letters to her mother; she cannot be goaded into speech; she is fighting a long delaying battle against absorption into his way of life as though she had not a tongue in her head. So the endless tirade goes on, while Cliff Lewis tries ineffectively to defend the battered, punched, browbeaten and trampled-on girl, who says nothing and does nothing in reply, but goes on ironing, ironing, with a look of blanched sorrow on her face, which is white and exhausted as if after a hundred sleepless nights, tormented by a hundred ceaseless headaches.

All this time – it is the greater part of the evening – Jimmy Porter, with his grievances, his anguishes, his angers, his injustices, and his cruelty holds the centre of the stage. Even in this part of the play Mr Osborne shows more than a flash of theatrical talent. His wit is often amusing and penetrating. The use of a trumpet off-stage is excellently contrived to create an atmosphere of breaking nerves. The third act beginning brilliantly repeats, with one vital difference, the opening of the first. But the inexhaustible outpouring of vicious self-pity comes near to wearying the audience's patience; and though Mr Kenneth Haigh plays Jimmy Porter with confidence and strength, he does so from the outside, as a continual flow of bitter rhetoric, not as the inevitable expression of a tormented spirit. There are episodes of whimsy that might have made Barrie blush and Jimmy's grievances are too rarely translated from words into concrete theatrical situations.

The audience has, however, the remedy in its own hands. It should do what audiences have always done with *Much Ado About Nothing*; that is, leave the chief characters alone, and concentrate on Benedick and Beatrice, the subsidiaries. Alison Porter is a subsidiary in *Look Back in Anger*; it is not she, but her husband, who throws into the past a maleficent gaze. But it is her endurance, her futile endeavour to escape, and her final breakdown which are the truly moving part of the play. The dramatist that is in Mr Osborne comes in the end to feel this himself, and it is to Alison, when at last she makes her heart-broken, grovelling, yet peace-securing submission, to whom the final big speech is given.

Hers is in its way a kind of victory; and because it is a kind of victory, it releases instead of depressing the spirit. To know when to give up the struggle, to realise when the battle no longer counts, this also is a sort of triumph. There is a poignant moment during the second act when Alison desperately cries, 'I want a little peace.' It is peace that she gets at the end, as Raskolnikov gets it when he ceases to maintain himself innocent. In this matter Mr Osborne's debt to his director, Mr Tony Richardson, and to Miss Ure, is immense. Miss Ure's especially is the long endurance, and the victory. In smaller parts Miss Helena Hughes and Mr Alan Bates are both very good. (Harold Hobson, in the *Sunday Times*)

'THEY are scum,' was Mr Maugham's famous verdict on the class of State-aided university students to which Kingsley Amis's *Lucky Jim* belongs; and since Mr Maugham seldom says anything controversial or uncertain of wide acceptance, his opinion must clearly be that of many. Those who share it had better stay well away from John Osborne's *Look Back in Anger* (Royal Court), which is all scum and a mile wide. Its hero, a provincial graduate who runs a sweet-stall, has already been summed-up in print as 'a young pup', and it is not hard to see why. What with his flair for introspection, his gift for ribald parody, his excoriating candour, his contempt for 'phoneyness', his weakness for soliloquy and his desperate conviction that the time is out of joint, Jimmy Porter is the completest young pup in our literature since Hamlet, Prince of Denmark. His wife, whose Anglo-Indian parents resent him, is persuaded by an actress friend to leave him: Jimmy's prompt response is to go to bed with the actress. Mr Osborne's picture of a certain kind of modern marriage is hilariously accurate: he shows us two attractive young animals engaged in competitive martyrdom, each with its teeth sunk deep in the other's neck, and each reluctant to break the clinch for fear of bleeding to death.

The fact that he writes with charity has led many critics into the trap of supposing that Mr Osborne's sympathies are wholly with Jimmy. Nothing could be more false. Jimmy is simply and abundantly alive; that rarest of dramatic phenomena, the act of original creation, has taken place; and those who carp were better silent. Is Jimmy's anger justified? Why doesn't he *do* something? These questions might be relevant if the character had failed to come to life; in the presence of such evident and blazing vitality, I marvel at the pedantry that could ask them.

Why don't Chekhov's people *do* something? Is the sun justified
in scorching us? There will be time enough to debate Mr
Osborne's moral position when he has written a few more plays.
In the present one he certainly goes off the deep end, but I cannot
regard this as a vice in a theatre that seldom ventures more than
a toe into the water.

Look Back in Anger presents post-war youth as it really is,
with special emphasis on the non-U intelligentsia who live in
bed-sitters and divide the Sunday papers into two groups, 'posh'
and 'wet'. To have done this at all would be a signal achievement;
to have done it in a first play is a minor miracle. All the qualities
are there, qualities one had despaired of ever seeing on the stage –
the drift towards anarchy, the instinctive leftishness, the automatic rejection of 'official' attitudes, the surrealist sense of humour
(Jimmy describes a pansy friend as 'a female Emily Brontë'), the
casual promiscuity, the sense of lacking a crusade worth fighting
for and, underlying all these, the determination that no one who
dies shall go unmourned.

One cannot imagine Jimmy Porter listening with a straight
face to speeches about our inalienable right to flog Cypriot
schoolboys. You could never mobilise him and his kind into a
lynching mob, since the art he lives for, jazz, was invented by
Negroes; and if you gave him a razor, he would do nothing with
it but shave. The Porters of our time deplore the tyranny of
'good taste' and refuse to accept 'emotional' as a term of abuse;
they are classless, and they are also leaderless. Mr Osborne is
their first spokesman in the London theatre. He has been lucky
in his sponsors (the English Stage Company), his director
(Tony Richardson), and his interpreters: Mary Ure, Helena
Hughes and Alan Bates give fresh and unforced performances, and
in the taxing central role Kenneth Haigh never puts a foot wrong.

That the play needs changes I do not deny: it is twenty minutes
too long, and not even Mr Haigh's bravura could blind me to the
painful whimsey of the final reconciliation scene. I agree that
Look Back in Anger is likely to remain a minority taste. What
matters, however, is the size of the minority. I estimate it at
roughly 6,733,000, which is the number of people in this

country between the ages of twenty and thirty. And this figure will doubtless be swelled by refugees from other age-groups who are curious to know precisely what the contemporary young pup is thinking and feeling. I doubt if I could love anyone who did not wish to see *Look Back in Anger*. It is the best young play of its decade. (Kenneth Tynan, in the *Observer*)

Look Back in Anger, which joins the repertory of the English Stage Company at the Royal Court Theatre, is a remarkable piece of writing by a new author, Mr John Osborne. His play is set on the seamy side of the Kingsley Amis world, his protagonist one of the modern self-destructive teddy-boy intellectuals, who can do nothing with his brains and education except rail against what present-day life offers him. As a play, *Look Back in Anger* hardly exists. The author has written all the soliloquies for his Wolverhampton Hamlet and virtually left out all the other characters and all the action. But in these soliloquies you can hear the authentic new tone of the Nineteen-Fifties, desperate, savage, resentful, and, at times, very funny. This is the kind of play which, for all its imperfections, the English Stage Company ought to be doing, and which those who cry out for writers in the theatre ought to support. I hope to discuss the play at the length it deserves next week.

If I were Mr George Devine I should regard *Look Back in Anger* as something of a test case. This is just the sort of play which the English Stage Company was created to produce; and it was created in the belief that a great capital like ours could produce an audience loyal and interested enough to invest a few shillings a week in supporting experiments like this one. If there is such an audience, let them show their interest by filling out the performances of this play. If there is not, let us all stop pretending there is, and complaining that no one comes along to do just what Mr Devine is now doing.

Of course, *Look Back in Anger* is not a perfect play. But it is a most exciting one, abounding with life and vitality, and the life it deals with is life as it is lived at this very moment – not a common enough subject in the English theatre. The three young people who are crowded together in a top flat in some Midlands town are being slowly destroyed. Jimmy Porter, the protagonist, is a brilliant young intellectual adrift, and since he can find no other way of using it, he is employing his intelligence to punish himself and everyone round him. It is a dazzling performance, and he knows it (he is not an attractive hero). It is also a monstrous one, and he knows that, too. But he can't stop it; the self-destroyers never can. He has seen through all the tricks of self-deception by which we people persuade ourselves that life is worth living, and debunks them in a brilliantly funny series of tirades. His is the genuinely modern accent – one can hear it no doubt in every other Expresso bar, witty, relentless, pitiless and utterly without belief. Since he cannot find himself a place, he must compensate by making fun of all those who can; and his wit bites home.

It is painful as well as funny, and someone must suffer for it, the one who is nearest, in this case his wife. She has had the misfortune to be better born socially than he and he uses this incessantly and brutally – but any other excuse would do. All she can do is suffer the assault, helped out by the inarticulate Cliff Lewis, the dumb and loyal friend who is always the necessary third in this kind of marriage. Mr Osborne understands some aspects of life deeply, and renders them truly, and one of his particular merits is to dare to go further in showing us the things that people do to one another than is usually revealed on the stage.

Not a pleasant play, then. The battle goes on repetitively in its squalid setting. The wife is temporarily driven out; her best friend replaces her, and she too gives up. There is not enough action and it is not all convincing. But what remains completely convincing is the mood and the contemporary language in which it is expressed. Mr Osborne's mistakes of construction are so howling that I am inclined to believe that we have all missed his intentions here. He is an actor himself, and must know that you can't keep building up expectancy for characters who never appear (unless their non-appearance is their point). Then he fails to place his hero's predicament on any dramatised motives. Motives are written into the text, true; but they are not working in it, fermenting it and aerating it. In the naturalistic form he has chosen (perhaps mistakenly), we inevitably ask questions which aren't answered. A sweet-stall, for instance, is such an odd choice of occupation for an intellectual *manqué* that we need an explanation. We need lots of other explanations, too, and feel cheated not to be given them. The biggest cheat of all is Mr Osborne's end. He has too successfully persuaded us of his hero's state of mind, to palm us off with a phoney reconciliation.

All the same, don't miss this play. If you are young, it will speak for you. If you are middle-aged, it will tell you what the young are feeling. It is particularly well acted by Mr Devine's resident company. Mr Kenneth Haigh's young intellectual completely convinced me; he missed none of the savage humour and was endlessly resourceful in getting variety. Above all he avoided, as the part demanded, drawing sympathy to himself. The sympathy goes to his wife, and Miss Mary Ure, dumbly taking it, gave one of her best performances; while Mr Alan Bates was admirably self-effacing as the third member of the *ménage*. Miss Helena Hughes and Mr John Welsh completed the strong cast. The true and vivid interpretation of the actors was the best of tributes to Mr Tony Richardson's intelligent direction. (T. C. Worsley, in the *New Statesman*)

IT has not been very often in recent years that we have seen a good first play by a young author on the London stage. Still rarer have been plays dealing convincingly with contemporary types and problems. It was, therefore, a pleasant surprise to encounter one at the Royal Court Theatre the other evening. John Osborne's play is about three subjects at once. As a basis there is the psychology of the modern romantic, of the young man who behind all his toughness and rudery is perpetually building idealised images of people and things, which they are unable to live up to and which then turn to bitterness within him. And his situation is made worse by the fact that, in the present-day world, there is no cause to which he can give himself wholeheartedly, no

centre on which he can concentrate his adolescent dreams. This
is the second theme of the play. In the Thirties Jimmy Porter
would have been a Communist and fought in Spain, but now
there is nothing for him but to work on a sweet-stall and relive
nostalgic memories of the time when there seemed to be something to believe in. Anarchism is, of course, a sterile attitude
except when it is held by the artist. Jimmy Porter is no artist.
One feels at the end of this play that he will talk and talk and talk
in his attic flat in an industrial town until he rots. It is immaturity that is his trouble. Emerging from extreme youth most
people accept the world and a few transcend it. He can do neither.
In this sense Mr Osborne's play is a tragedy.

The actual action of the play is centred around Jimmy's
relationship with his wife Alison, and his anarchism here develops
into the familiar pattern of Strindberg's love/hate relationship
between the sexes. Deeply in love, the young couple are perpetually inflicting wounds on each other, until eventually the wife
feels she can bear no more. Her place in the *ménage* is taken by
her friend, Helena Charles, who also feels the same ambivalence
in her love for Jimmy, moving in her case from hatred to love.
Mr Osborne brings out very well the appalling side of all this
self-destruction which continues until the calm of desolation is
established in the last act and the tragedy of Jimmy Porter is
paralleled by that of his wife.

Out of these complex psychological and social themes
Mr Osborne has made a powerful and sombre play relieved every
now and then by flashes of humour. The dialogue is always tense
and witty, though there are speeches (in particular some of
Jimmy's monologues) which could do with cutting. This,
however, is a very minor fault beside the outstanding merits of
the work. At the Royal Court it is very well performed. Kenneth
Haigh makes an obsessive job of Jimmy, while Mary Ure, as his
wife, shows how good an actress she can be. Helena Hughes and
Alan Bates bring accomplished support to the two main characters,
while Tony Richardson's direction makes the whole thing as
fast and as tense as it needs to be. Mr Osborne was well served
by his producer and actors, but the principal credit is the writer's

– a fact which justifies the policy pursued by the English Stage Company. (Anthony Hartley, in the *Spectator*)

JOHN OSBORNE, the author of *Look Back in Anger*, makes it clear from the start that he intends to kick us in the teeth, and go on kicking us. 'Squeamish, are you?' we can hear him saying, 'you just wait!' So he draws liberally on the vocabulary of the intestines and laces his tirades with the steamier epithets of the tripe butcher. His hero, who for most of the evening is roaring his contempt for the middle and upper classes and indeed for any orderly plan of living, is a very tiresome young man, an exhibitionist wallowing in self-pity. He bullies and humiliates his wife, whose prim parents have not unnaturally opposed the marriage, and when his social rage is temporarily exhausted he weeps at the infinite sadness of his life. If you ask why he behaves like a spoilt baby, the answer is hard to find, except that this is Freud's centenary and I suspect Mr Osborne of an over-dose of Tennessee Williams; all that can be claimed in the man's defence is an unhappy childhood, but otherwise, in spite of having a degree behind him, he has chosen to quarrel with everyone, run a sweet-stall and live in an animal way in an abysmally sordid one-room flat.

The very odd thing is that Mr Osborne seems to expect us to sympathize with this creature, as if he were a reasonable representative of a betrayed and bewildered generation. Anyone less deserving of sympathy I cannot imagine; self-pity hardens the most charitable heart. One is sorry for his wretched little wife, pulverized by his verbal artillery (one began to feel bruised oneself), and delighted when she leaves him; but I could have smacked her for her final grovelling return, in hysterical renunciation of all the creeds black-listed by bed-sitter nihilism. Is this supposed to be a splendid gesture on behalf of the self-oppressed? In any case it is no end to the play, for the whole silly cycle of torture and collapse will clearly begin again.

This is a first play, and if I have been hard on it it is because Mr Osborne has not done justice to his own powers. He has a good turn of wit and phrase, and an ability, when he is not overwriting, to express himself with force. There are moments here, swamped by bitterness and hysteria, that might have been moving; and though the dialogue holds up the action by trying to be too clever, it is not without quality. Having got this gall out of his system he should write a more interesting play.

The heavy burden of almost constantly addressing a public meeting is carried by Kenneth Haigh, slightly monotonously but with spirit. Pale and crushed, Mary Ure dumbly conveys the nervous strain of living with a masochist, and there is a good performance by Alan Bates as the simpleton friend who stands by faithfully. Helena Hughes plays the upright visitor who loathes her host and then, when his wife leaves him, suddenly becomes his mistress. One moment she is smacking his face in fury, the next, to our great astonishment, they are locked together. I felt she would never have stayed five minutes in such a zoo, but Miss Hughes went some way to persuading me. (Eric Keown, in *Punch*)

PART TWO

Writings by John Osborne

THE WRITER IN HIS AGE (1957)

THE *London Magazine* invited nine authors to answer the questions printed below. They were asked not to consider themselves obliged to answer the questions in order or precisely point by point, but to give their views as a general statement.

During the Thirties it was a widely-held view that poets, novelists and playwrights should be closely concerned in their writing *with the fundamental political and social issues of their time. Since then, the degree of an imaginative writer's necessary engagement with the age in which he lives has been the subject of constant debate with very varied conclusions. Do you think that today, in 1957, it is a valid criticism of such a writer to say that (1) he appears indifferent to the immediate problems of human freedom involved in, say, the Rosenberg case and the Hungarian revolution; (2) he shows no awareness (a) of the changes that have been caused in our social structure and our way of life by, for instance, the development of atomic weapons and the levelling down of classes through discriminatory taxation, nor (b) of the challenges to our conception of human existence caused by recent discoveries in such sciences as biology, astronomy and psychology; (3) his novel, play or poem could,* judged on internal evidence only, *have been written at any time during the last fifty years?*

JOHN OSBORNE *answered as follows:*

In attempting to answer these questions, I can only answer them as a writer working in the theatre. I can't make judgements about

the tasks of poets and novelists. Their problems are quite different
from mine, and, anyway, I don't know enough about them.
Besides, I think it will save a little confusion. The answer to
question (1) of this questionnaire contains the answer to the
other questions. Of course most writers appear to be indifferent
to the problems of human freedom, like Hungary and the Rosen-
bergs. The reason for this is, I believe, that most writers find it
difficult to be engaged in the problems on their door-step. If you
are surrounded by inertia at home, it is not so easy to get all
steamed up about what is going on in Central Europe or America.
A man with a mysterious pain in his gut, or a spot on his lung,
can summon up some interest in a campaign against cancer or TB.
At least he can give it some thought because it is there somewhere
with him. It wasn't so difficult to make up your mind about
which side of the barricades you were voting for, when men
were standing about on street corners all over England, and
nobody was doing anything about it. People were being thrown
on the economic ash-can all around you. It only needed a very
reasonable eyesight to see it and a very reasonable decency to
stand up and shout about it. Now, the ash-can is very different, so
different that it's difficult to recognize. Now that the man on the
street corner is taking home twelve or fifteen pounds a week, his
family get 'free' medical treatment, 'free' school meals (paid for
principally by the working classes themselves in taxes), he seems
to have become a pretty contemptible creature. His poor over-
taxed betters are keeping this greedy monster, and they turn
their favourite Sunday newspaper into a sort of posh Peg's
Paper, telling everyone about it – like a lot of well-bred Angry
Young Chaps. And these people are *really* angry. They see
themselves being eaten alive by this ignorant creature, with his
telly and his pools, swallowing up all culture, all good manners,
all decent behaviour. Why, they even send his sons to these redbrick places for him, while *they* struggle and make do without
domestic help in order to send their own lads to the only places
that haven't been levelled down, thank God! And then these
ungrateful little bastards shout their loutish heads off and bite
the hand that feeds them.

You have a situation, then, in which most ordinary working people are materially better off than at any time in history, and this has been achieved – inevitably – at the expense of a sizeable minority and to them the monster on the street corner begins to look a pretty ugly customer. He is powerful, he still looks fairly gentle (after all *he's* British too) but he seems quite oblivious to the resentments around him. This isn't the kind of atmosphere that produces the heart-searchings and the gestures of the 'thirties. The monster has been allotted a very comfortable, reasonably clean ash-can. He is still sitting on the pile of rotting culture, the half-chewed bones of symbols and debased values that should have been washed away long ago.

Now, my own sympathies are quite unequivocal in all this. They are all with the monster because I think he has been dumped on an ash-can as dirty and as dangerous as the old one. It may be a failure in my own sensibility that I can't be very moved by the plight of a man who feels that he has to spend half of his £2,000 a year on educating his children, but I can't. He is simply trying to keep them out of the monster's reach, and, at the moment, he doesn't seem to manage too badly. The idea seems to be that if you shower the monster with enough cultural, emotional and spiritual rubbish, he will sit quite happily on a great soft, cosy mountain, and never notice the stink. You hurl it at him from your cinemas, and TV sets, and magazines and newspapers and then dodge away quickly, holding your nose, and hoping desperately that one day, he may even bury himself in it and disappear. Anything to avoid the odium and the bother of trying to speak to him in a language which you can both understand. Any writer who works in the theatre, and most of all, in films or TV has got to try and find this language. He has got to start trying to clear away the rubbish, and not worry about getting his hands dirty, or losing his friends because they decide he's not only slightly mad, my dear, but getting smelly as well. I believe a writer's job today is quite clear and staggeringly difficult. It is to try and get over to as many people as possible, to the ash-can. To do it without compromise and patronage. The individual writer has just about everything against him, all the

big boys who owe it to themselves to keep the ash-can going.
But somebody's got to make a start.

THE EPISTLE TO THE
PHILISTINES (1960)

TIMOTHY, an apostle of our Gracious Lady by the Will of God,
to the sweet, lovely, loyal people of Great Britain, and to the
faithful wherever they may be.

Grace be to you and peace from Our Gracious Lady and all
princes and others who have smiled on us from carriages and
high places.

I rejoice to bring you tidings of humble men elevated, for it is
now said by their fruits ye shall know them and not by their
roots.

Inasmuch as the old and once established religion was
unsatisfying to the people, it being steeped in some parts in
morality and man's relation to the universe, the new gospel has
been pronounced and taken root long since.

The people are glad and satisfied for their lives are now rich
and full of meaning.

They need not to think of the morrow nor to think at all,
for they see clearly as through a glass coach.

Since the power comes not before the glory, through your
Simply Divine Rights the power shall be yours and the glory
also.

This is the doctrine that shall be spread abroad, for it is
revealed of Grace, and shall be known as Justification through the
Defender of the Faith and the Ministry of Works.

I tell you: the glory shall be yours and the power also. It shall
be yours; the richness, the abundance and the honour.

You shall have rank, privilege, the love even of our Dear
Madam Grace and Favour in whose blessed bounty all our well
set up hopes shall finally lie.

For Her sake you shall diligently come and go forth, you itinerant painters and wall paper pickers;

You gown sellers, fashion setters, you ploy makers and play fakers;

You poets and Rolleiflex flickers;

You breathy column sisters and microphone prelates; you dancing rogues and morning coat vagabonds;

You hushers and high mushers, you guff vendors and you friendless ones also;

All you obsequious, envious ones; you tendentious leader men;

You knights and cringers; you pinched conformers; and indeed all you exquisite things.

You shall be called henceforth the New Set, for many are sybarites but few are chosen;

The Queendom shall be yours and it will come soon; and the day shall come when we are all Queens, each and every one of us.

Therefore rejoice, take heart and be diligent. Thy Queendom Come.

THAT AWFUL MUSEUM (1961)

In an odd way the theatre, I believe, has had more influence on English life in the last five years than the cinema or the novel. Its contribution to television has been tremendous, and it's revitalized a lot of other things. Even newspapers, to a small extent; and the language, too, to a lesser degree. I don't think that we're quite as American-orientated as we were, or as London-dominated either – that's very important – and the theatre can take a big share of the credit. It's helped to create a new context of English life. And now the same kind of small revolution is taking place in films.

The big danger in the 1960s is the formation of a new theatre Establishment. That, I feel, is the objection to the National

Theatre, where all the safest talents will be busy creating some
kind of awful museum. It seems to me like the idea of building
a new Royal Academy. Simply on the basis of one's experience
of English life, one knows that it would be the smaller, safer
people who would be in charge. That's the way it always works,
unfortunately. Perhaps I *am* a pessimist, but *I* think I'm being
realistic about it, and I should hate to see some of the good
talents wasted in creating a waxwork museum. It would give
some actors better parts and guaranteed employment, but that
seems to me such a minimal return for erecting yet another
institution. I agree that hypothetically the National Theatre
might be stimulating to me and other dramatists if a really free
and new stage was built there: except that one doesn't know
what the context of power would be, and whether one would
want to work in it. For example, the theatre that I most enjoy
going to in London is the Mermaid, because the building has all
the virtues that one demands of a playhouse. It's comfortable,
it's hospitable, it has a simple excitement about it, and you feel
that you're in a place that has something to do with the twentieth
century instead of being shut up in an Edwardian box. Technically,
it's interesting, too. But the fact that I enjoy going to the
Mermaid and looking at that stage doesn't necessarily mean that
I could see myself wanting – or being invited – to write for it.

There's a danger, too, that the Establishment of the 1960s may
try to promote a synthetic version of the really new theatre, with
all its teeth drawn. Safe, apparently high-minded middle-brow
plays which make all the *gestures* but are really not very
different from the old Shaftesbury Avenue models. We've seen
some of those already: both eyes are on one side of the stag's face,
but it's still the same Landseer product in disguise. At the moment
most of the old-style commercial managers haven't the talent or
the imagination to construct a formula for themselves, however
synthetic. They're very worried about the pressures they feel
bearing in on them, but for the most part they're completely
unable to respond to those pressures. One of the best things the
English Stage Company has done is to make a new kind of
management possible.

What do I want for the theatre of the 1960s? First, decent conditions for people to work in, and decent theatres built by architects who know something about it. But what I would like most of all – although of course it's not something you can legislate for – is to see artists in the theatre being allowed to *play* at their work. Everything has to be so serious and specific all the time, and people are continually under the pressure to improve on their last work, to do it perfectly every time, to create a success. The element of *play* seems to have gone out of life, but artists should have the right to relax, to be frivolous, to indulge themselves in their work. The people who do it most obviously are painters. You can see very graphically the *play* in some of Picasso's work, handling bits of newspapers and bottles with the frivolity of a deeply serious, dedicated, marvellous artist. I think we should all be allowed that kind of scope for a complete artistic freedom, so that sometimes we don't have to please audiences or please critics or please anybody but ourselves. It's possible to write for yourself and to write for a few people at the same time. It's also possible to write for yourself and write for everybody. But it's not my job *as a dramatist* to worry about reaching a mass audience if there is one, to make the theatre less of a minority art. So much of that, in any case, depends on other factors like new buildings with good restaurants, service and other amenities. If you're going to do what other people think or say you ought to do, it's a waste of time. Ultimately, after all, the only satisfaction you get out of doing all this is the satisfaction you give yourself.

I'm not particularly interested in the shapes of the new stages. Certain plays work in arena stages, and others don't. I've seen a wonderful production of *The Iceman Cometh*, but *Les Nègres* in the round doesn't work at all. I myself have never felt tempted to write for that form. Somehow I'm just not attracted to it, and I have reservations about the open stage, too. In my plays I like to establish a kind of remoteness between the actors and the audience, which I only like to break at certain times, and I can do that in the picture-frame stage. It's true that I felt restricted by it in *The Entertainer*, but one can find different ways of breaking out without using different stages. Although *Look Back in Anger* was a formal, rather old-fashioned play, I think that it broke out by its use of language – Harold Pinter does that now. Of course, the Royal Court as a building is cramping and inhibiting. It diminishes most plays, especially those on a bigger scale. For example, *The Entertainer* was much more successful at the Palace, which is a much bigger theatre. To some extent you're inhibited by knowing that you're writing for a specific stage, at least initially. But you can't allow yourself to be too conscious of that, and think 'Oh, I won't do that because it can't be done at the Court.' You must go on and do it. Certainly, I don't really visualize a picture-frame stage when I'm writing. If I think of anything, I think of a theatre that doesn't exist, one that combines the intimacy of the Court with the grandeur of a circus. I'd love to write something for a circus, something enormous and immense, so that you might get a really big enlargement of life and people. What's so boring about television is that it *reduces* life and the human spirit. Enlarging it is something that the theatre can do best of all.

That's one reason why I'm not interested in writing for television. Economically, it has nothing to offer, considering the amount of work involved. And most of the people on the executive level are dim, untalented little bigots. They create a great mystique around the technicalities of television, which are really immensely simple. Anybody with any creative or imaginative sense can easily master them – or ignore them. But I enjoy film work. A certain amount of organizing activity has always appealed to me, and I find that it's an outlet for those feelings. It gives me the illusion that I can *do* things, and I find that stimulating. But it's still true that the theatre comes first for me, as a writer. As an actor? Well, I always enjoy acting, and if I were offered a really good part I'd be tempted. But I've never taken myself seriously as an actor, and neither has anyone else. It would really be a bit self-indulgent to do it any more! Of course, when I'm writing I see all the parts being played beautifully by me, to perfection!

It's difficult to pinpoint just how *Luther* started. It's been brewing over a long period. I wanted to write a play about religious experience and various other things, and this happened to be the vehicle for it. Historical plays are usually anathema to me, but this *isn't* a costume drama. I hope that it won't make any difference if you don't know anything about Luther himself, and I suspect that most people don't. In fact the historical character is almost incidental. The method is Shakespeare's or almost anyone else's you can think of. I've already begun my next play, but I don't want to talk about it now. I'm not really equipped to talk about what I'm doing and what I've done – especially about the things that are furthest away in time. I daren't pick up a copy of *Look Back* nowadays. It embarrasses me.

A LETTER TO MY FELLOW COUNTRYMEN (1961)

THIS is a letter of hate. It is for you, my countrymen. I mean those men of my country who have defiled it. The men with manic fingers leading the sightless, feeble, betrayed body of my country to its death. You are its murderers, and there's little left in my own brain but the thoughts of murder for you.

I cannot even address you as I began as 'Dear', for that word alone would sin against my hatred. And this, my hatred for you, and those who tolerate you, is about all I have left and all the petty dignity my death may keep.

No, this is not the highly paid 'anger' or the 'rhetoric' you like to smile at (you've tried to mangle my language, too). You'll not pour pennies into my coffin for this; you are *my* object. I am not yours. You are my vessel, you are *my* hatred. That is my final identity. True, it will no doubt die with me in a short time and by your unceasing effort.

But perhaps it could be preserved, somewhere, in the dead

world that you have prepared for us, perhaps the tiny, unbared spark of my human hatred might kindle, just for the briefest moment in time, the life you lost for us.

I fear death. I dread it daily. I cling wretchedly to life, as I have always done. I fear death, but I cannot hate it as I hate you. It is only you I hate, and those who let you live, function and prosper.

My hatred for you is almost the only constant satisfaction you have left me. My favourite fantasy is four minutes or so non-commercial viewing as you fry in your democratically elected hot seats in Westminster, preferably with your condoning democratic constituents.

There is murder in my brain, and I carry a knife in my heart for every one of you. Macmillan, and you, Gaitskell, you parti-cularly. I wish we could hang you all out, with your dirty wash-ing, on your damned Oder-Neisse Line, and those seven out of ten Americans, too. I would willingly watch you all die for the West, if only I could keep my own miniscule portion of it, you could all go ahead and die for Berlin, for Democracy, to keep out the red hordes or whatever you like.

You have instructed me in my hatred for thirty years. You have perfected it, and made it the blunt, obsolete instrument it is now. I only hope it will keep me going. I think it will. I think it may sustain me in the last few months.

Till then, damn you, England. You're rotting now, and quite soon you'll disappear. My hate will outrun you yet, if only for a few seconds. I wish it could be eternal.

I write this from another country, with murder in my brain and a knife carried in my heart for every one of you. I am not alone. If *we* had just the ultimate decency and courage, we would strike at you – now, before you blaspheme against the world in our name. There is nothing I should not give for your blood on my head.

But all I can offer you is my hatred. You will be untouched by that, for you are untouchable. Untouchable, unteachable, impregnable.

If you were offered the heart of Jesus Christ, your Lord and your Saviour – though not mine, alas – you'd sniff at it like sour offal. For that is the Kind of Men you are.

Believe me,

In sincere and utter hatred,

Your Fellow Countryman,

JOHN OSBORNE

Valbonne, France

ON CRITICS AND CRITICISM (1966)

LET me say this first: I am no scab and no critic either, thank God. While Mr Alan Brien, the theatre critic of this newspaper, is on holiday no management, no actor and no writer in English need expect or fear abuse, heavy patronage or boredom from these columns. For once I am working for money only.

After nearly twenty years of agitating and trying to create affray from within my own profession, I still cannot contemplate going over to Them. By Them I mean the acknowledged enemy, the critics, most particularly the daily newspaper critics, acknowledged cheerfully and openly by all but a few sleepy pear managements and some truckling actors.

Theatre critics should be regularly exposed, like corrupt constabularies or faulty sewage systems. Indeed, as the structure of institutional theatre grows, I would employ gentle, subsidised chuckers-out so that most daily critics might be barred from openings altogether, along with actors' agents and boxes of chocolates. If they would only heed my advice, the National Theatre would engage someone to write a regular consumer's guide to critics. It could be an amusing addition to an already attractive and handsome programme. I could contribute myself now and then, naming names, and there are others who could do so with even more skill and relish. Mr Lindsay Anderson, for example. Or that theatre's own dramaturge, Kenneth Tynan, now gainfully and usefully employed after a distinguished career as a critic himself.

My own attitude to most critics is clear and entirely reasonable. It is one of distrust and dislike based on predictability and historical fact. I regard them as something like kinky policemen on the cultural protectionist make, rent collectors, screws, insurance men, Customs officers and Fairy Snowmen. One should simply not open one's door to them. The reason for this is fairly simple. They consistently threaten my livelihood and have done so for the past ten years of my working life. Whatever success or reputation I may have earned is due to a few isolated writers on the theatre, the wet noses of news editors, and the blessed alchemy of word of mouth.

Imagine the situation in any other trade. Building, perhaps. Hirelings are engaged who glory in their technical ignorance and might as easily be writing about dog racing – and possibly enjoy it better. They are then encouraged to deprive you of your living, threaten your future and your children's daily sliced bread. Do they expect to be loved or even liked? It is high time for acrimony to out.

For my last play, *A Bond Honoured*, I was paid £250. For a year's work or so this is less than my wife and I were awarded by the National Assistance Board 13 years ago. Last year I was obliged to invest over £7,000 of my own money in my own play, *A Patriot for Me*, mainly because of polite threats of police prosecution from St James's Palace.

No, let us be open. Distrust and dislike is general and mutual. Most of the people who are hired to write about the theatre are bored by it, or, like the critic of the *Daily Express*, sit longing for salt beef sandwiches and the forgetfulness of Fleet Street after the ball is mercifully over. Intellectuals detest and despise it openly.

Let me give an example. A Mr John Weightman, who I believe is a professor of – predictably – French Literature, is encouraged to write in – predictably – an intellectual magazine called *Encounter*, a publication in which superior brains bitch each other either frontally or indirectly month after month. It's an astonishing performance. One wonders how people can consistently sustain such self-parody, like the B.B.C. Critics, so long enjoyed as the middlebrow's Workers' Playtime. Mr Weightman says that Noël Coward cannot act. Which is rather like saying that Marlene Dietrich can't sing. Mr. Coward, like Miss Dietrich, is his own invention and contribution to this century. Anyone who cannot see that should keep well away from the theatre.

No, I will name no more names, though it is a temptation. I will just say this to critics: learn to dislike yourselves. Learn what Professor Heer calls 'loving openness'. Look to your lives, whatever they may be like. Sometimes it is hard indeed to believe you have ever been instructed in any pain, absurdity or distress. Think of the theatre as an ordeal, as an act of love is an ordeal, as an historical incitement. As one of the few acts of communion left to us. Imagine that this may be the last time the Host is raised before your eyes.

Remember also that theatrical ideas are theatrically expressed and not in the literal-minded manner of literary weeklies. They are not to be recognised like intellectual mottoes tattooed on random pieces of sculpture. They are organic, and when they work they can be seen to be working. Critics should have the charity of poets, like Sir Philip Sidney, who could write such a line as 'My heart was wounded with his wounded heart'. Fire can still burn when all the matter's spent and we live in such a time, and performing and writing plays often seems an act like writing on tombstones to those who do it.

Do not pretend either that you don't ever discuss the play in the interval and cull fish heads of attitudes and jokiness from one another. You have been observed too often by too many witnesses. My friend Mr David Merrick, a non-drinker and obsessive theatre-bar goer, would sign an affidavit to this at any time. So would I. Another thing: it may be comforting to know that you are unloved and unwanted but you would be wrong to congratulate yourselves. You could well become obsolete. You still need to amuse and inform some of the time. Some of us no longer have that obligation, even though we may occasionally observe it.

PART THREE

Critical Studies

John Russell Taylor

JOHN OSBORNE (1963)

WHATEVER may be said about John Osborne's subsequent career, at least no one can deny that *Look Back in Anger* started everything off: after a slightly shaky beginning it became the first decisive success in the career of the English Stage Company and established the Royal Court as the London home of young drama. Although the lead in these matters had passed elsewhere in later years, and 'the Osborne generation' proved only the first of several waves, 8 May 1956 still marks the real break-through of 'the new drama' into the British theatre, and Osborne himself remains, one way and another, one of its most influential exponents, as well as representing for the general public the new dramatist *par excellence*, the first of the angry young men and arguably the biggest shock to the system of British theatre since the advent of Shaw. And this in spite of the inevitable difficulties of following up a sensational début with something which guarantees that the first sensation was not merely a freak success or the one work of a one-work writer.

Though *Look Back in Anger* was the first of Osborne's plays to reach the London stage, it was not by any means his first written; he admits to 'several' works unpublished and unperformed as well as *Epitaph for George Dillon*, written in collaboration with Anthony Creighton, which came earlier but was performed later, and an early piece which contributed some material to *The World of Paul Slickey*. He had also already had two plays performed out of town, *The Devil Inside Him* in Huddersfield in 1950 and *Personal Enemy* in Harrogate in 1955. The first, written in collaboration with Stella Linden and revived at the Pembroke, Croydon, in 1962 as '*Cry for Love*, by Robert Owen', is a strange melodrama about a Welsh youth whom the

villagers think an idiot and his relations a sex-maniac because he
writes poetry; his talents are recognized by a visiting medical
student, but meanwhile he is constrained to kill a local girl who
attacks his idea of beauty by attempting to pass him off as the
father of her child. More characteristic was *Personal Enemy*,
written with Anthony Creighton, about the reactions of a
soldier's relatives and friends when he refuses to be repatriated
from his captivity in Korea; the play apparently suffered at the
time from wholesale deletions demanded by the Lord Chamberlain, including a whole homosexual strand in the plot. But *Look
Back in Anger* it was which provided the first type-image of the
new drama, and which has dogged its author ever since, so it
seems inevitably the right place to start. When it was first
performed Osborne was twenty-six, an actor with some years'
experience in provincial repertory, notably at Ilfracombe and
Hayling Island, and familiar to regulars at the Royal Court in
small parts, though he says that he never took himself seriously
as an actor, and neither did anyone else.

Looking back on *Look Back in Anger*, it is a difficult but
necessary exercise to try and see it through the eyes of its first
audience. . . . Osborne himself has recently characterized it as
'a formal, rather old-fashioned play', and the description is
not unfair, though it should, of course, be read in the light of
his accompanying statement that he dare not pick up a copy
of the play nowadays, as it embarrasses him. Certainly there is
nothing much in the form of the piece to justify so much excitement: it is a well-made play, with all its climaxes, its tightenings
and slackenings of tension in the right places, and in general
layout it belongs clearly enough to the solid realistic tradition
represented by, say, *The Deep Blue Sea*.

No, what distinguished it as a decisive break with Rattigan
and the older drama was not so much its form as its content: the
characters who took part in the drama and the language in which
they expressed themselves. Though Jimmy Porter and his milieu
seem, even at this short distance of time, as inescapably 'period'
as the characters in *The Vortex*, quintessentially 'mid-fifties', it
was precisely the quality of immediacy and topicality which

makes them so now that had the electrifying effect in 1956: Jimmy was taken to be speaking for a whole generation, of which he and his creator were among the most precocious representatives, since it was essentially the post-war generation they represented, those who had, like Lindsay Anderson, 'nailed a red flag to the roof of the mess at the fort of Annan Parbat' to celebrate the return of a Labour government in 1945 and then gradually became disillusioned when a brave new world failed to materialize. Most of the people who felt this way were inevitably in their middle to late thirties in 1956, but with Osborne as a figurehead they were all cheerfully labelled 'angry young men' and Jimmy Porter was linked in a rather improbable twosome with Amis's Lucky Jim as the cult-figure of the younger generation.

The main usefulness of Jimmy Porter in this guise is that he is the stuff of which perennial rebels are made; though it is more difficult now than it was five years ago to see him as heroic, there is no denying the truth of the picture as a permanent human type – the self-flagellating solitary in self-inflicted exile from the world, drawing strength from his own weakness and joy from his own misery. He is, we gradually learn, a university graduate and an enormous cultural snob (only the safe classics and the most traditional jazz, only good books and 'posh' Sunday papers), but he lives in a tumbledown attic flat in a drab Midland town and makes his living by keeping a sweet stall in the market. Everything in his life dissatisfies him, and the tone of his conversation (which is mainly monologue anyway) is consistently one of railing and complaint. The principal sufferer from all this is his wife Alison, whom he cannot forgive for her upper-middle-class background and whom he constantly torments in order to extract some reaction from her, to bring her to her knees, while she, having discovered that her only defence is imperturbability, refuses as long as she can to react. And so they rend each other, under the sympathetic eye of Cliff, the helpless *tertium quid* in this strange *ménage à trois*, until a fourth, Alison's actress friend Helena, arrives. Helena, with her air of being 'the gracious representative of visiting royalty', soon makes the situation intolerable by her very presence, and packs off Alison, who is expecting a baby and has not told Jimmy, to her home and family before herself falling into Jimmy's arms at the end of the second act.

In the third act Jimmy turns out to be settled fairly happily with Helena, as far as he can be happy with anyone – partly, it seems, because she stands up to him rather more (like most bullies in sexual situations, Jimmy appears basically just to want bullying back) and partly because he is bound to her by nothing more complicated than lust. When Cliff announces that he thinks he should leave, Jimmy more or less admits these two possibilities in the play's most familiar pronouncement:

> It's a funny thing. You've been loyal, generous, and a good friend. But I'm quite prepared to see you wander off, find a new home, and make out on your own. All because of something I want from that girl downstairs, something I know in my heart she's incapable of giving. You're worth half a dozen Helenas to me or to anyone. And, if you were in my place, you'd do the same thing. . . . Why, why, why do we let these women bleed us to death? Have you ever had a letter, and on it is franked 'Please Give Your Blood Generously'? Well, the Postmaster-General does that, on behalf of all the women in the world. I suppose people of our generation aren't able to die for good causes any longer. We had all that done for us, in the thirties and forties, when we were still kids. There aren't any good, brave causes left. If the big bang does come, and we all get killed off, it won't be in aid of the old-fashioned, grand design. It'll just be for the Brave New Nothing-very-much-thank-you. About as pointless and inglorious as stepping in front of a bus. No, there's nothing left for it, me boy, but to let yourself be butchered by the women.

It is not, however, Helena who finally reduces him, but Alison, returned after losing her baby. When Helena wants to extract herself from the painful situation Jimmy dismisses her with:

> It's no good trying to fool yourself about love. You can't fall into it like a soft job, without dirtying up your hands. It takes muscle and guts. And if you can't bear the thought of messing up

your nice, clean soul, you'd better give up the whole idea of life, and become a saint. Because you'll never make it as a human being. It's either this world or the next.

Then he rounds on Alison:

Was I really wrong to believe that there's a – kind of – burning virility of mind and spirit that looks for something as powerful as itself? The heaviest, strongest creatures in this world seem to be the loneliest, like the old bear, following his own breath in the dark forest. There's no warm pack, no herd to comfort him. That voice that cries out doesn't *have* to be a weakling's, does it?

But she for once has an answer:

I was wrong, I was wrong! I don't want to be neutral, I don't want to be a saint. I want to be a lost cause. I want to be corrupt and futile! Don't you understand? It's gone! It's gone! That – that helpless human being inside my body. I thought it was so safe, and secure in there. Nothing could take it from me. It was mine, my responsibility. But it's lost. All I wanted was to die. I never knew what it was like. I didn't know it could be like that! I was in pain, and all I could think of was you, and what I'd lost. I thought: if only – if only he could see me now, so stupid, and ugly and ridiculous. That is what he's been longing for me to feel. This is what he wants to splash about in! I'm in the fire, and I'm burning, and all I want is to die! It's cost him his child, and any others I might have had! But what does it matter – this is what he wanted from me! Don't you see! I'm in the mud at last! I'm grovelling! I'm crawling! Oh, God –

Faced at last with a really effective example of his own handiwork, Jimmy quails, and at the last he and Alison are united again in their idyllic dream world of bears and squirrels, content, perhaps, never to make it as human beings in the real world around them.

One of the most fascinating things about *Look Back in Anger* is the divergence between Osborne's conscious intentions, as conveyed in his comments and stage directions in the printed text, and what actually emerges in performance. This applies, particularly, of course, to the character of Jimmy, and indeed it

is arguable that the force and intensity of the play derive mainly
from the author's shifting, ambivalent love–hate relationship
with his hero. In the stage directions criticism direct or implied
abounds. For example, at the beginning Jimmy is described as 'a
disconcerting mixture of sincerity and cheerful malice, of tenderness and freebooting cruelty; restless, importunate, full of pride,
a combination which alienates the sensitive and insensitive alike.
Blistering honesty, or apparent honesty, like his, makes few
friends. To many he seems sensitive to the point of vulgarity.
To others, he is simply a loudmouth. To be as vehement as he is
is to be almost non-committal.'

That does not sound particularly heroic, and the impression is
fostered by the running commentary of stage directions throughout: 'Jimmy is rather shakily triumphant. He cannot allow himself
to look at either of them to catch their response to his rhetoric...';
'He's been cheated of his response, but he's got to draw blood
somehow'; 'Jimmy watches her, waiting for her to break';
'Jimmy enters . . . he is almost giddy with anger, and has to
steady himself on the chair . . .' There are constant indications
of his neurotic determination to establish and keep his supremacy
in any situation, inventing trouble if there is none lying around
in order to do so, his hysterical persecution of Alison, his childish
petulance. Indeed, the image which constantly emerges is that
of the spoilt, difficult child, convinced that any world not run
entirely for his convenience must of necessity be out of joint,
and in need of nothing more than a good slapping down (which
would square with the theory that his misfortune sexually is
that he has coupled with a doormat when what he really longs for
is a strict disciplinarian nanny-substitute).

And yet somehow this is not quite what comes over in the
play on stage. For one thing it is called *Look Back in Anger*, not
Look Back in Petulance, and both the most familiar interpreters
of Jimmy (Kenneth Haigh in the original stage production,
Richard Burton in the film) have been stocky, substantial, heroic
figures rather than the weedy neurotics one might fairly cast in
the role. For another, Osborne has, consciously or unconsciously,
provided a complete cover for the heroic interpretation: what

by the less ideal view would be merely excuses (everyone is out of step but our Jimmy) become if one looks at it from the other point of view genuine reasons: there are no great causes left, the world is all wrong, and it need not be just the weakling who cries out against it; Jimmy is the saintlike witness to right values in a world gone wrong, the mouthpiece of protest for a dissatisfied generation. And finally, what really makes this interpretation stick in the playgoer's mind is the burning rhetoric of his great tirades: even if their motivation is to be found in petty personal disputes and minor skirmishes in the battle of the sexes, once Jimmy gets going they generate their own force and conviction; those around him put up with him and listen entranced instead of briskly telling him to shut up and not be so silly, and his very real personal dynamism and magnetism come over to the audience as they do to the other characters on the stage. The only mystery is, Why should someone so forceful remain so impotent? And there we come back at once to the answer he himself provides: it is the deficiencies of the modern world which have made him so.

Look Back in Anger is demonstrably a muddled play – muddled, that is, in what it has to say and the way it says it – but this naturally is only a very minor consideration: a play is about people, not necessarily about ideas, and what matters is not that Jimmy is a mass of contradictions (most of us are), but that Osborne has managed to make them into a convincing dramatic representation of a complex human being, and one who offered a rallying-point for a number of people from the post-war generation who felt that the world of today was not treating them according to their deserts. It may be argued, though, that Osborne achieved this partly at the expense of his other characters: to build up Jimmy he has had to a certain extent to scale down the rest, and paradoxically (or perhaps it is not so paradoxical, as we shall see) the only other person in the play who measures up to him in solidity and conviction is Alison's father, the Colonel – partly, no doubt, because he is the only one we never see with Jimmy and subjected to Jimmy's normal barrage.

It is, however, a general trait in Osborne's work that he tends to sympathize with his hero in his writing to such an extent that the other characters are made to capitulate to him almost without a struggle and the scope of genuine dramatic conflict is thereby reduced. The remarkable thing about *Epitaph for George Dillon*, the only earlier work we know in anything like its original form, is that this is not entirely so, since though it has an angry young hero, not only is he given an adversary worthy of him, but in the end doubt is more decisively cast on his probity and worth than is ever permitted in *Look Back in Anger* (despite the stage direction referring to Jimmy's 'apparent honesty'). This may, for all we know, be the influence of Osborne's collaborator on this play, Anthony Creighton . . . : certainly the character of Ruth, though somehow never quite of a piece with the rest of the play (how, one finds oneself asking, could she possibly have sprung from the background attributed to her?), is in her own terms decidedly well drawn, and the head-on collision between them in the second act, when each digs too close to the other's soft centre for comfort and harsh truths emerge on both sides, generates a sort of excitement not found elsewhere in Osborne's work. That has its excitements, too, of course, but they are the excitements of the monologue and the tirade, the solitary orator and his captivated audience, not those engendered by the clash of two equally powerful personalities on one small stage.

George, the central character of the play, is an actor and writer; he is sponging off the Elliotts, an easygoing, simple family living just outside London, and though the father does not care for him he is adept at getting his own way with the mother, whom he reminds of her dead son, and Josie, the hard, stupid daughter. Professionally he is a failure, or, as he prefers to put it, he is waiting for success; he is a recognizable Osborne hero, restless and dissatisfied – a rebel who knows what he is against without being very clear what he is for. He pities himself, situated in a hostile and uncomprehending world, but unlike Jimmy Porter he has, every now and then, enough penetration to doubt whether he is worth pity; is he a real artist deserving of sympathy in the torments an artist conventionally undergoes, or is he just a confidence trickster who usually tricks himself as well? In Ruth, Mrs Elliott's left-wing intellectual sister, he finds someone oddly like himself in certain respects; an ex-Communist who has just broken with the party after seventeen years, soon after casting off her lover of six years because she discovered their relationship was built on cheap lies, she is uncertain of herself, uncertain of her value to herself and others, dissatisfied with her position, but not ready to make a change.

In their great confrontation, which might be a love scene but somehow does not turn out that way, they strip each other bare of comfortable pretences, and George comes to admit openly and even sincerely (as far as anything he says is not part of his incessant self-dramatizing) that he may be living on an illusion, that he may not have talent after all – 'But do you know what is worse? Far, far, worse? . . . Having the same symptoms as talent, the pain, the ugly swellings, the lot – but never knowing whether or not the diagnosis is correct. Do you think there may be some kind of euthanasia for that? Could you kill it by burying yourself here – for good?' Whether or not this is possible, in the last act he sets out to do it: he rewrites his play so that it rakes in money on tour in the provinces as an adults-only shocker, recites his own epitaph to Ruth (who does not even hear it out) to mark his own spiritual death, and at the end of the play seems all set to marry Josie as soon as he has divorced his wife and live an ordinary suburban life, trying to kill the spark inside him which he can never for a moment confidently accept as the real thing.

By virtue of its balance, its ability to see round the central character and offer him some genuine competition without sacrificing at all the passionate rhetorical drive of the dialogue, *Epitaph for George Dillon* still remains the most wholly satisfactory of the plays Osborne has worked on. This, coupled with the fact that it was staged after *Look Back in Anger*, tended at first to obscure the lines of Osborne's development. But not for long, and Osborne, never at a loss for words to explain himself, was not slow to tell us why his style was changing: it was the first impact of Brecht on his consciousness which made him see the light and begin to find the limitations of realism (against which he was already chafing in *Look Back in Anger*) too impossibly restricting. In *The Entertainer*, his next play, the influence of Brecht is very marked in a number of incidentals, though one would guess that, at that time at least, he had not fully grasped what the epic theatre was about (the totally misconceived film version, scripted by Osborne himself, which tries to transplant all the least realistic sections unchanged into a setting of documentary realism, would tend to support such an opinion).

In effect, the structure of the play presents a series of realistic scenes – more realistic, perhaps, than anything in *Look Back in Anger* – dropped quite arbitrarily into an 'endistancing' epic framework. On the realistic level we have the story of Archie Rice, a corny, fading comedian playing in a holiday show called *Rock'n Roll New'd Look* at a large seaside town. He is, we gradually learn, a hollow man, unable to make real contact with anyone – his father Billy, whom he loves but who maddens him, his wife, whom he pities, or his children, two of whom we meet, the shy, easygoing Frank and Jean, who is intense and rather priggishly left-wing. He uses his comic persona to ward off anyone who may want to look him straight in the face and, cornered as he is, he can be completely unscrupulous – he sets up an affair with a young girl so that her parents will finance his new show, and when that fails because Billy goes and tells them that he is married with three grown-up children he allows Billy, one of the few survivors from the great days of music-hall, to return to the stage to recoup the family fortunes. His son Mick, fighting at Suez, is killed, and for a moment it touches him, but only for a moment; he is dead almost beyond rousing – the portrait, perhaps, of Jimmy Porter twenty years later, or George Dillon in ten years, when the effect of their capitulation is complete and visible.

Encasing these scenes is a framework of supposed music-hall numbers, performed mostly by Archie, which make an oblique but unmistakable comment on the main action, their burden being that the world is rotten, riddled with apathy, and the theatre, as we see it and as it is summed up in the person of Archie, is the symbol of this state of decay: audience and actors are equally inert. As Archie puts it drunkenly to Jean just before the news of Mick's death arrives:

You see this face, you see this face, this face can split open with warmth and humanity. It can sing, and tell the worst, unfunniest stories in the world to a great mob of dead, drab erks and it doesn't matter, it doesn't matter. It doesn't matter because – look at my eyes. I'm dead behind these eyes. I'm dead, just like the whole inert, shoddy lot out there. It doesn't matter because I don't feel a thing, and neither do they. We're just as dead as each other.

'Anger' is, in fact, again the keynote of Osborne's comment on the modern world (the label of the 'angry young man', now fortunately almost dropped from currency but in its time much overused, still has that grain of truth in it) – Jimmy's statement that there are no good causes left to die for finds its exact visual parallel and commentary, for instance, in the staging of Archie's song 'Thank God I'm Normal', with its pseudo-patriotic verse ('if we all stand By this dear old land The battle will be won') illustrated by a blowsy nude Britannia wearing only a helmet. But, of course, if the modern world is to be castigated it must be by comparison with something else, some other era, and here we come straight to the central contradiction in Osborne's work: what is looked back on with nostalgia is precisely the era of Edwardian settlement and complacency which in other contexts would be looked back on with the fiercest anger. We noted in *Look Back in Anger* the surprising fact that the only character apart from Jimmy who is allowed his say and some measure of genuinely independent existence is Alison's father, towards whom Jimmy's own reactions are ambiguous: Alison says she thinks that in spite of everything Jimmy rather likes him, though he is obviously in many ways the representative of everything Jimmy is against. And the reason for this is clear enough, on a moment's consideration: at least in their heyday Alison's father's generation knew where they were, what standards their lives

were ruled by, and where their duty lay (or so, at least, it now
seems); they had causes to die for and even if they were wrong
they had a certain dignity. Their security in an apparently secure
world is eminently to be envied by someone, like Jimmy, who
finds no certainty anywhere, outside himself or within.

Similarly in *The Entertainer* there is at least one point of
reference in a sympathetic member of the older generation, Billy
Rice. With Archie, as with George Dillon, we can never be sure
how far he is really a victim of the world around him and how far
he is the creator of his own situation: basically, it seems, he
never was talented and he could never have done much better
than he is doing now, catering for the decadent tastes of modern
audiences (and not, apparently, doing that very well, since even
on this level he fails to bring them in); his one moment of
realization, when he heard a negro woman singing in a way
which told him, for the moment, that 'it didn't matter how much
you kick people, the real people, how much you despise them, if
they can stand up and make a pure, just natural noise like that,
there's nothing wrong with them, only with everybody else', has
served merely as a painful reminder, a glimpse of a lost Eden he
could never attain and to which no one holds the key any more
('I don't suppose we'll ever hear it again. There's nobody who
can feel like that'). But Billy was great, and is great still, a
survivor from the heroic past of popular entertainment's heyday
in the Edwardian music-hall, now gone for ever.

In his note to the printed text Osborne says: 'The music-hall
is dying, and, with it, a significant part of England. Some of the
heart of England has gone: something that once belonged to
everyone, for this was truly a folk art.' Significantly, Osborne is
here writing of something, like the Edwardian splendours of
India, which he cannot possibly remember himself and which
becomes therefore, for him, a romantic legend to be longed for
as an alternative to the indecisions and false values of modern
life. The intelligent political man of left-wing sympathies in
Osborne tells him – and us – that it was the faults in this ante-
diluvian world which brought our world into existence, but the
incorrigible romantic looks back admiringly, and these plays are

the battlegrounds (hence much of their excitement) on which the two Osbornes fight it out.

More sympathetic elders occur in Osborne's next work, *The World of Paul Slickey*, where, in fact, they are almost the only people towards whom even a spark of sympathy is permitted. This 'Comedy of Manners with Music' is generally, and not unfairly, regarded as Osborne's most complete failure; critically and commercially it certainly was, and even allowing for an exaggeration of hostility in proportion to the exaggeration of preliminary hopes for it after *The Entertainer*, it is difficult to find anything good to say for it now. It was based, apparently, on an unproduced script from before *Look Back in Anger*, and was Osborne's first attempt at a genre for which he is totally ill-suited, the social satire. The liveliest passages of Osborne's plays may often involve, or appear to involve, social criticism, but if we look closer it is clear that the criticism, such as it is, is never based on a close examination of its object (hence the curious interchangeability, in different contexts, of his objects of detestation and devotion); it is all entirely subjective, a volley of grape-shot flying off in all directions in which the person who discharges it counts for much more than his nominal targets (that is to say, while some hits, most misses, but this is not vitally important to our judgement of the plays, because they are so devised that it is the force rather than the accuracy of the attack which counts for most). But satire calls above all for a degree of objectivity, if only so that the satirist can size up his object's weak points and aim directly at them; the blunderbuss of open anger must be replaced by the pearl-handled automatic of considered irony. But this is the last thing we would expect from Osborne: in *The World of Paul Slickey* anything and everything comes under the same erratic fire, mountains and molehills are greeted with equal fury, and by the time we are through savaging the church, the aristocracy, the gutter Press, those masculine women and feminine men (as well as their more bigoted opponents), the success ethos, the tawdriness of teenage tastes in music, the sentimentality of the woman's magazine, supporters of blood sports and corporal punishment, anti-semites, anti-negroes, and anti-anti-H-bomb demonstrators, and just about every other imaginable *bête noire* of the discontented intellectual, we are tempted to turn Osborne's own words against him: 'To be as vehement as he is is to be almost non-committal.'

And, in fact, about one or two of his central targets Osborne is ultimately curiously non-committal. 'Paul Slickey' himself, the gossip-columnist hero-villain who personifies the workings of the bitch-goddess success, proves to be dishearteningly soft-centred: he does not really like his job, he has moments of doubt and depression, he sees himself already as much more the victim of the machine than its manipulator; in a word, he is sentimentalized and the blame for him and his like put on an undefined 'them' who have forced him into the rat-race. Similarly Father Evilgreene, the sinister priest with his parody ritual (seldom, incidentally, can satire have been quite so heavy-handed and basically innocuous) turns out after all the to-do not to be a real priest at all, so that what we may have thought daringly directed against religion turns out simply (and safely) to be directed at imitation religion. And, as we have already remarked, the two embodiments of the privileged, aristocratic tradition which seems to be intended as one of the play's main targets, Lord and Lady Mortlake, turn out in fact to be the most amiable and sympathetic of all the characters, figures of sense and dignity who have strangely survived into a mad and frenzied world; Evelyn Waugh himself could hardly have put the case for aristocracy more unequivocally.

As the plot (which is reduced to a minimum anyway) progresses all these characters are introduced against the background of a surprisingly well-kept stately home, owned by Jack Oakham's ('Paul Slickey's', that is) father-in-law Lord Mortlake; Lord Mortlake does not know that Oakham is Slickey, hence one slight line of plot, but most of the story concerns the complicated pattern of adultery woven by Jack, his wife Lesley, his sister-in-law Deirdre Rawley, and her husband Michael, with the aid of Gillian Giltedge-Whyte, a debutante, Terry Maroon, a rock'n'-roller, and Jo, Paul Slickey's secretary – all leading to the conclusion that the only escape from marital boredom is a change of sex. There are fourteen songs, confirming what we had already gathered from *The Entertainer*, that lyric-writing is not Osborne's forte: they include 'Bring Back the Axe', 'The Mechanics of Success', 'The Income Tax Man', and 'I Want to Hear About Beautiful Things', the titles of which are all sufficiently self-explanatory.

Considerably more interesting, though treated to a reception almost equally disastrous, is Osborne's first (and to judge from his subsequent comments on the matter his last) television play, *A Subject of Scandal and Concern*. The history of this was long and involved, and it was offered round a number of the independent companies before being finally accepted by the B.B.C., who agreed to perform it as written, while the other companies had required rewriting and adaptation. The reason for their worries about it became clear when the play was performed and published, for, in fact, it turns out to be not so much a play as an illustrated lecture – an effect which the B.B.C. production intensified by substituting for the costumed narrator of the printed text, placed physically in the prison setting in which much of the drama takes place, an extra-smooth John Freeman playing the television uncle for us against an anonymous studio background. The story that the narrator has to tell is interesting enough: the prosecution of George Holyoake, the last man to be imprisoned for blasphemy in this country. Holyoake was a socialist lecturer who was put on trial in 1842 for saying, in response to a question at a public meeting, that he did not believe in God. In the play we see a little of his relationship with his wife, a careful reconstruction of his trial, in which he conducted his own defence despite a speech impediment and an almost total ignorance of the law, and his later experiences in prison, where he remains enigmatically impassive despite the news of his friend's recantation before death, his wife's reproaches over his daughter's death, and the fervent exhortations of the chaplain; he ends, as he began, very much a man of mystery, rising to eloquence only at his trial, when for the moment he loses his impediment in defence of his own convictions.

All this is handled in a straightforward, not particularly imaginative fashion, and the meat of the play comes mainly in the narration. The Narrator is always there at the viewer's elbow, telling him what has just happened and explaining what is about to happen, drawing the moral or pointing out sententiously that no simple moral can be drawn. This is 'endistancement' with a vengeance, since any attempt on the part of the play to stand on its own feet is immediately stamped on by a prompt return to the lecture-room, and while this may prevent one from becoming improperly involved in the action it runs the severe risk of preventing one also from becoming even properly interested in it. Again, one suspects Osborne's Brechtian enthusiasms have contributed to the method employed, but the Narrator's introduction (modified slightly in the version acted) reads like a parody of Brecht's ideas, with a hint of disdain for the audience very personal to Osborne thrown in for good measure:

Good evening. I am a lawyer. My name is not important as I am not directly involved in what you are about to see. What I am introducing for you is an entertainment. There is no reason why you should not go on with what you are doing. What you are about to see is a straightforward account of an obscure event in the history of your – well, my – country. I shall simply fill in with incidental but necessary information, like one of your own television chairmen, in fact. You will not really be troubled with anything unfamiliar. . . .

Similarly with his readings from *The Cheltenham Chronicle* of the day about the part of the meeting we have just witnessed, his imparting of the information that 'Mr Holyoake had finished, his voice notably stronger and his impediment astonishingly improved' when we have just seen and heard this very event, and his pretentiously throwaway conclusion (slightly shortened in performance):

This is a time when people demand from entertainments what they call a 'solution'. They expect to have their little solution rattling away down there in the centre of the play like a motto in a Christmas cracker. For those who seek information it has been put before you. If it is meaning you are looking for, then you must start collecting for yourself. And what would you say is the moral then? If you are waiting for the commercial it is probably this: you cannot live by bread alone. You must have jam – even if it is mixed with another man's blood. That's all. You may retire now. And if a mini-car is your particular mini-dream, then dream it. When your turn comes you will be called. Good night.

(Note, incidentally, the decay of Osborne's earlier angry eloquence into a merely mannered abruptness of delivery applied to words which are more than ever gesture without real meaning.)

What Osborne is after in this use of narration seems clear enough, but the weakness of *A Subject of Scandal and Concern* is still the same as that of *The Entertainer*: that his adoption of Brechtian processes in only half-hearted. What happens in both of them is that the framework of comment – the music-hall songs, the narration – is in one convention and the scenes contained by that framework are in another: the same *verismo* as *Look Back in Anger*. This persistent failure to evolve an integrated new dramatic technique to replace the old lent a particular interest to the appearance of his second historical play, *Luther*; would he in this, tackling for the first time a theme right away from contemporary realism in the medium in which he was most at home, the stage, manage at last to find a satisfactory new form for his work?

The answer is still yes and no, but the reasons for this evasion are unexpected. First it must be said that the play as a whole corresponds very closely in dramatic method to the reconstructed scenes in *A Subject of Scandal and Concern*: the historical material is straightforwardly presented on the whole, with Luther's own words used whenever possible (as Osborne and his supporters rapidly pointed out to the tender-minded who quailed at the dramatist's apparent obsession with constipation and defecation). Moreover, it is not 'Brechtian' in the senses conventional to the English theatre, being neither dressed up with songs and dances *à la* Theatre Workshop nor equipped with a ubiquitous audience-representative in the shape of a Common Man (as favoured by such examples of Brecht tamed and commercialized as *A Man for All Seasons*): 'narration', in fact, is reduced to a brusque announcement from the stage of time and place. Here the model seems to be rather the direct chronicle of *Galileo*, in which man as an individual and man in society are held as far as the spectator's interest is concerned in an edgy balance. Brecht manages to preserve the balance very effectively between the inner forces which drive Galileo on and the social forces (Church and State) which hold him back. In Osborne the balance is less satisfactory, since so much time is spent on the 'psychological' material early on – Martin's obsession with his own sinfulness, with the sinfulness of merely being alive, and his relations with his father, whom he loved, and his mother, who beat him – that by the time this all bears fruit in his rebellion and heresy, and he moves out (like Galileo) into the world of repressive social forces (emanating, like those that opposed Galileo, from the Vatican), there is not enough room left to deal with them properly.

From Act II, Scene 4, at the end of which Luther nails his theses to the church door at Wittenberg, the issues involved are scurried over in unseemly haste, with a rather feeble scene of disputation between Luther and Cajetan, the papal legate (which again demonstrates Osborne's deficiencies when a conflict of equals rather than a tirade to a captive audience is called for, since, though apparently engaging in a discussion, Luther and Cajetan never really interlock so that one answers the other; their 'dialogue' turns out, in fact, to be two monologues skilfully intercut), and another, even weaker, showing Pope Leo about to go hunting, to take care insufficiently of the theological side before we get to the Diet of Worms. Then we jump four years to learn something, but not to the uninitiated enough, about the intervening period of war and Luther's apparent betrayal of the peasants, though what happened and why remains obscure (even with the scene between Luther and the Knight, not in the original text, inserted to clarify matters). The closing scene, in which we see Luther at home two years later with his wife and son, returns unashamedly to the personal with, finally, a note of nostalgia which should by now be familiar to us in Osborne's work:

Luther, himself the instigator of a period of unrest and unsettled values, looks back to an earlier, happier day:

A little while, and you *shall* see me. Christ said that, my son. I hope that'll be the way of it again. I hope so. Let's just hope so, eh? Eh? let's just hope so.

Well, what about *Luther*? Does it really represent, as one critic opined, 'the most solid guarantee yet given of Mr John Osborne's dramatic stamina'? Alas, although after the relative failure of *The World of Paul Slickey* and *A Subject of Scandal and Concern* one had hoped that it would provide a reasonably clear answer, there is nothing for it but to hedge again. However, one or two pointers there are. It is noticeable, after the extreme thinness of the material in *The World of Paul Slickey*, that both *A Subject of Scandal and Concern* and *Luther* are historical reconstructions relying closely for their material and even for their dialogue on the documentary sources. This seems to suggest a drying-up, perhaps temporary, of Osborne's inventive faculties at least in so far as they concern the creation of new characters and plot-situations; instead he is turning to plots and characters already in existence. The failure of *The World of Paul Slickey* and *A Subject of Scandal and Concern*, followed by the popular and critical success of *Luther*, suggests also that after some fumbling he has mastered the technique of handling pre-existent material efficiently, to form a play which if not completely satisfactory in detail is at least well enough written and interesting enough in its material to provide a generally satisfactory evening's theatre.

I do not think anyone would deny that *Luther* is that – especially with the magnetic personality of Albert Finney in the title role – but it would surprise me if anyone on mature consideration can find it as intense, as eloquent, as personal, as – to bring out the key word here – as *felt* as *Epitaph for George Dillon*, *Look Back in Anger*, or *The Entertainer*. It is a good, sensible, commercial piece of work, spiced with enough anger and naughty words to establish it as representative of a later generation than, say, Rattigan's *Adventure Story*, but basically it is not so different from *Adventure Story*, or for that matter *A Man for all Seasons* or Anouilh's *Becket*. It has been popular, as they (the last two, at any rate) were popular, and on the whole it deserves its popularity. But the most positive new discovery about Osborne it offered us was that he was not just the primitive we had feared he might be – inspired or nothing; he could turn his hand to play-writing simply as a craft and turn out something perfectly presentable. But equally, taken in conjunction with the two previous plays, it did make us wonder whether, barring any sudden unforeseen transformation, we would have to say good-bye to Osborne the innovator and greet instead Osborne the careful craftsman. To such wonderings Osborne's subsequent work offers little in the way of definite confirmation or denial. His next work for the theatre was in any case fairly slight after the elaborate and ambitious *The World of Paul Slickey* and *Luther*, a sort of intermezzo in his career produced by the pairing of two contrasted, though both primarily comic, one-act plays, *The Blood of the Bambergs* and *Under Plain Cover*, in a double bill under the general title *Plays for England* (1963). Development in various directions they certainly showed, but neither could be said to provide a startling revelation. *The Blood of the Bambergs* is by general consent the least satisfactory of all Osborne's plays: a clumsy attempt at the sort of satire for which he showed himself signally unfitted in *The World of Paul Slickey*, it concerns the last-minute substitution at a royal wedding of an Australian press photographer for the royal groom, who has just been killed in a road accident and whom the photographer by a curious coincidence happens to resemble like a twin brother (the dead prince's father, it seems, had known the photographer's mother not wisely but too well). The subject-matter caused a certain preliminary fluttering in the dovecots (a satire about a royal marriage with a photographer – how daring!) but in fact the result proved to be perfectly harmless and acceptable; indeed, with its accent on the fact that royalty's life is no bed of roses and its final demonstration that even the interloper is of blood royal and therefore fitted by birth for the life he is to lead, it ends up curiously like a conservative tract, with most of its venom reserved for the press and television journalists who cheapen the image of royalty. Perhaps Osborne himself more than half believes, to quote one of his less happy would-be epigrams, that 'An orb in the minster is better than a monster in orbit'.

The second play in the bill, *Under Plain Cover*, is much more interesting. It is tempting to see it as a sort of fourth act to *Look Back in Anger*, in which Jimmy and Alison have tired of Bears and Squirrels and gone on to a few more sophisticated party games. The married couple this time, Tim and Jenny, lead perfectly ordinary lives except for their odd hobbies, which consist of acting out a variety of sado-masochistic fantasy situations in clothes which they receive 'under plain cover'. Sometimes one dominates, sometimes the other: she may be a strict, no-nonsense nurse and he a cringing patient, or he a heartless employer and she a down-trodden maid, and so on. They put real enthusiasm and imagination into their charades: when she wonders, for example, why the maid she is playing doesn't leave if she is so badly treated, he decides that it is the 1930s and there is nothing else for her except the bread-line; in the second scene there is a long nonsense-fantasy about knickers (a fetish they share) in which every conceivable description is applied to them, including a number from reviews of Osborne's earlier plays ('the total gesture is altogether inadequate'). And as a result of their fantasies and fetishes they are happy, well-adjusted, efficient parents and, as far as the outside world is concerned, just what the postman calls them, a nice ordinary couple. Indeed, absolutely they are just that: they have a marriage which works; they merely externalize changes in the emotional balance of power and make positive use of them where others experience them only as a bugbear and a puzzlement.

So far, so good: an interesting point interestingly made, if perhaps at excessive length, in two scenes where one would be enough. But at this point Osborne seems suddenly to be confronted with the need to make his sketch into a play, and the ghost of Paul Slickey enters, slightly disguised as Stanley, a snooping, cynical reporter. When he starts interfering, Osborne's own obsession with the evils of gutter journalism takes over and the play goes to pieces: Stanley unearths evidence that Tim and Jenny are, unknown to themselves, brother and sister, separates them, gets Jenny remarried and even brings Tim in as a loving brother to the wedding reception. But the marriage does not last: sometime later Tim and Jenny are apparently together again in their semi-detached, and Stanley, a broken man, knocks on their door, desperate to talk to them. But there is no answer....

If *The Blood of the Bambergs* is easily the feeblest work Osborne has yet allowed to reach the stage, *Under Plain Cover* does show some signs of a recovery; at least for its first half it finds a new subject, or anyway shows an old subject – the relations of husband and wife – in a new light. It is, in parts, the most interesting thing Osborne has written since parts of *The Entertainer*, but as a whole it just does not work; in the second half he dissipates most of the effect he has spent the first half building up (drawing heavily, by the way, on an actual case related in Harry Proctor's book *Street of Disillusion* for the incest theme and the role of the reporter). Osborne the innovator is present – though the subject is less daring than it would have been some years before, and one cannot help thinking that Pinter would do it better – and Osborne the careful craftsman conspicuous by his absence. Evidently it is too early to write Osborne off altogether, but on the other hand it is difficult to feel much confidence in what he will do next. If it takes up the line hinted at in the first half of *Under Plain Cover* it just might be remarkable; but with *The Blood of the Bambergs* before our eyes too, any hopes we may nurture are bound to be mixed with more than a little foreboding.

INADMISSIBLE EVIDENCE (1964)

IT has already become more or less a commonplace of criticism to say that *Inadmissible Evidence* is John Osborne's best play. I am not going to argue with that judgment: it seems to me that this time Osborne has found, perhaps as a result of thought, perhaps by a lucky chance in the material he has chosen to make his play out of, a solution to most of the problems which previously tended to snarl up his plays. For example, to take the basic one: his constant trouble with dialogue, or perhaps I should say with duologue. Only in the middle act of *George Dillon* is there anything approaching a genuine, unrigged, head-on clash between two equally matched characters who actually connect at several vital points – and there it is impossible for an outsider to tell how much the collaboration with Anthony Creighton had to do with this. Elsewhere Osborne's forte has always been impassioned monologue, carried along by the power of its own rhetoric and cheerfully unconcerned with what was going on around.

The trouble is that monologue of this sort is always difficult to accommodate in normal dramatic form. In *Look Back in Anger*, Jimmy monologuises endlessly and, rather unbelievably, everyone else sits round for most of the time and lets him; he is a stunning talker, admittedly, but not that stunning, and the effect is weakened because in the context (of what Osborne himself has called 'a formal, rather old-fashioned play') it is necessary that the other characters should not be quite so infatuated as the dramatist obviously is with the sound of his own protagonist's voice. Osborne's later plays have found no very satisfactory way out of this dilemma – think, for instance, of *Luther*, which works best when Luther is permitted to deliver his sermons entirely without interruption. But in *Inadmissible Evidence* Osborne has at last stumbled on an elementary truth: that his trouble in making characters connect arises primarily from the fact that what really interests him, anguishes him indeed, is the non-connection of people; it is – oh dear that one should have to come back to that most hackneyed piece of critical shorthand – failure of communication. It is as though this has always been his subject, but that up to now he has not fully understood what he was doing or wanted to do; now that he does, the effect is shattering.

For, critical cliché or no critical cliché, failure of communication, failure to connect, is still a perfectly viable dramatic subject; a subject, after all, is as good as the intensity of a writer's reaction to it allows it to be. In this new play there is no doubt about the vividness and intensity of Osborne's vision: he achieves a degree of imaginative identification with his hero (is 'hero' the *mot juste* here? Yes, in spite of everything I think it is) unequalled in his work since *Look Back in Anger*. The agony of the hero concerned, Bill Maitland, comes from his gradual, inexorable realisation that the world and he are parting company. He is fortyish, apparently well-preserved and well-off, a solicitor with a slightly unsavoury business (mainly divorces) which seems to run itself fairly well, with a weather-eye cocked for the Law Society; he has a wife, a daughter and a mistress; and he is hovering on the verge of a complete breakdown. The world, it seems, is conspiring to ignore his existence: his friends and associates turn away from him, taxis for hire take no notice of his attempts to hail them, people he is talking to on the telephone hang up on him in mid-sentence, or at least he is obsessed with the fear that they may have, that he may be talking on and on to the unresponsive air.

And for the most part, as it happens, he is – not particularly on the phone, but just in general. His employees in the office throw up their eyes – it's just him, carrying on again – and don't take a blind bit of notice; his clients burble on about their own problems, sublimely unaware how beside the point his responses are; his daughter, when she comes to visit him, stands wordless and reactionless throughout his great tirade and leaves without opening her mouth. Osborne has at last discovered the profound truth that nobody really listens to anybody, and least of all do they listen to those who most imperatively require their attention, their imaginative participation – in life, that is; on stage the reverse is the case, because our imaginative participation, our mere listening, does not immediately involve us in consequences in the world of action; we have only to listen, we don't have to *do* anything. That is why, when we saw everyone on stage being profoundly affected by Jimmy Porter, we did not quite believe it; the spectacle of nobody at all being affected by Maitland, on the other hand, is all too painfully believable. We all begin to wonder uneasily just how far our lives depend on the good will of others.

'Tu parles, tu parles, c'est tout ce que tu sais faire,' as Zazie's parrot would no doubt remark. But it is not quite all that Maitland knows how to do. He can suffer, for example, as well as talk about suffering; and he can, maybe, die. For *Inadmissible Evidence* is one of a group of works about people trapped, at the end of their tether, which have scattered through theatre and cinema in the last couple of years. As it happens, it is least like the one it has been most compared with, *After the Fall*; compared with that monumental, monstrous piece of self-justification disguised as True Confessions, this really is a confession. Though the old Osborne knack of telling us the worst about a character and yet still somehow leaving us on his side is still clearly in evidence in his treatment of Maitland, it is not unfairly done; we really are told the worst, and yet we are drawn unavoidably into Maitland's own faltering concern for himself, his feeling – which is the feeling of all of us – that for all his faults he has not quite deserved whatever it is that is in the process of befalling him.

Much nearer in every way to Osborne than *After the Fall* are Louis Malle's film of *Le Feu Follet* and Fellini's $8\frac{1}{2}$. Both give us the same feeling of identifying willy-nilly with an obviously far from estimable central character, and the parallels in subject-matter and even in form with the Fellini film are often so close that I suspect some immediate influence (perfectly proper and highly fruitful, let me add) of the one on the other. Osborne's hero, like Fellini's, is fortyish, quite successful in his career, enviably successful with women, equipped with a wife, a mistress and all the casual encounters anyone could desire; and like Fellini's Guido, Maitland is nevertheless at the end of his tether, searching hopelessly for a way out, a magic key to the door into the secret garden (represented perhaps in each case by youth and innocence, or rather spontaneity: Claudia in $8\frac{1}{2}$, Maitland's daughter Jane in *Inadmissible Evidence*); both are plagued by dreams full of obscure humiliation; both are losing their grasp on external reality (few things are more impressive in the Osborne play than the way in which reality gradually, almost imperceptibly slips from Maitland's, and our, grasps as little by little the passage of time blurs, characters fuse and merge into each other); and both reach the verge of suicide, if neither quite crosses over. One would not have thought of Fellini and Osborne as being particularly like-minded, and yet in these, perhaps their key works, the similarities are quite startling.

After all this it seems a trifle ungracious to come to the reservations. However, I don't have very many. I thought that the opening dream sequence, in which Maitland is on trial for exhibiting an unspecified obscene object (presumably himself) and tries fumblingly to defend himself, could with advantage be compressed and concentrated; and I am not at all clear how the episode in which he listens to the story of a homosexual client – well done though it is in itself – fits into the rest of the play; the women seeking divorce are clearly various aspects of Maitland's own unseen wife, but what does the homosexual represent in this otherwise intensely subjective play? As for the performance, again I have some slight reservations. . . . But about Nicol Williamson in the uniquely taxing role of Maitland himself there can be no reservation at all: this is one of the great performances in the modern English theatre, and even were the play infinitely less exciting in itself, would make the whole evening eminently worth while.

Katherine J. Worth

THE ANGRY YOUNG MAN (1963)

THE theatre, Shaw once said, does not 'develop'; its future can only repeat its past. Dramatic art will occasionally receive a 'germinal impulse', and one such he believed his own plays to have provided for the London theatre of the eighteen-nineties.[1] From this impulse sprang the realistic social drama which flourished for its most fertile years in the first decade of the twentieth century, taking root at the Royal Court Theatre in Sloane Square during the Vedrenne–Barker seasons of 1904–7.

Fifty years later, as Shaw had anticipated, the once lively young realistic drama had become stale and tired, the impulse appeared to have spent itself. A new 'germinal impulse' seemed to be needed, to stimulate the growth of quite a different kind of play. Impulses from abroad, notably from America, France, and Germany, were already being felt, but, curiously enough, the first play to achieve fame for the second major experiment at the Royal Court Theatre was not an experimental play. John Osborne's *Look Back in Anger*, produced there on May 8, 1956, was a 'fourth wall' realistic play, technically no different from such a play as Galsworthy's *The Silver Box*, which had been shown in the same theatre in 1906.

What then was the reason for its tremendous impact on audiences everywhere? One answer, swiftly supplied by the play's first reviewers, was the immediacy of its subject-matter. Osborne astonished and fascinated by his feeling for the contemporary scene, and the mores of post-war youth, by his command of contemporary idiom, and his tart comments on subjects ranging from the 'posh' Sunday newspapers and 'white tile' Universities to the Bishops and the Bomb.

The one thing the realistic drama cannot afford is to be out of date. Osborne brought it up to date, and, simply by restoring its proper qualities, seemed in 1956 to be doing something revolutionary, so remote from the facts of modern life had English realism become. He demonstrated in *Look Back in Anger* that the realistic form had not necessarily played itself out, that English drama was no longer, in Arthur Miller's phrase, 'hermetically sealed off from real life' and that there might yet be a second flowering of the plant germinated by Shaw. Within a few months of the play's production the televised performance had sent audiences crowding to the Royal Court Theatre and the *Observer* was holding a competition for new work of the same quality. The demand for truly realistic plays of contemporary life was shown to exist.

During its first six years the English Stage Company continued to rely heavily upon Osborne, half of its total income from sale of rights during this time deriving from his plays. But there was no lack of new playwrights to form what eventually came to be recognised by a title already applied to painting, the 'kitchen sink school'. As the first and most celebrated writer of the new order, Osborne soon found himself labelled. The phrases 'angry young man' and 'kitchen sink' became almost obligatory in reference to his work, and in some ways they were, of course, justified.

Yet the description of Osborne as a 'social realist' is misleading. His characters are highly critical of society and their criticism is so forcibly expressed as to make his plays seem more like Shaw's 'unpleasant' plays or Galsworthy's 'slices of life' than they really are. But in comparison with Shaw's concentration of dramatic interest on social problems in such plays as *Widowers' Houses*, Osborne's handling of social themes seems decidedly haphazard. This is not because he lacks the skill to marshal them differently, but because they are not, for him, of first dramatic importance. Most of the earlier realistic playwrights were dramatising social questions in order to stimulate social conscience: they had a 'palpable design' upon their audience and this was often the inspiration of the play. When Shaw wrote about the new 'problem play' in 1895,[2] he recognised that even the best of the kind would be 'as flat as ditch-water when *A Midsummer Night's*

Dream will still be as fresh as paint', but this seemed to him unimportant in comparison with the 'work in the world' that such plays would have done.

Look Back in Anger does not come into the category of 'didactic, realistic' plays, Shaw's own description of *Widowers' Houses*. Osborne is not concerned with social theories and panaceas. Social questions loom large in his plays only as they are imaginatively apprehended by his characters: they do not form the action. In his essay of 1895, Shaw had envisaged some such process coming about: the sheer size of modern societies and the pressure exerted by modern methods of communication would, he conjectured, produce 'a steady intensification in the hold of social questions on the larger poetic imagination'. The 'larger poetic imagination' is not to be confined by the topical: in Osborne's plays so far there can in fact be seen a significant movement away from such confinement. The result of this is not a decreased relevance to the life of our time: *Luther* has as much light to cast on characteristically modern problems of belief as *The Cocktail Party*, despite the surface modernity of Eliot's play.

It may well be asked what evidence of the 'larger poetic imagination' there is in Osborne's plays. The evidence in *Look Back in Anger* is certainly incomplete, but there are already indications in the striking rhetorical power of the play that here is an imaginative vitality going beyond that commonly associated with the realistic prose drama. In re-experiencing the plays of Galsworthy, for example, one is often reminded of Synge's description of writers who deal 'with the reality of life in joyless and pallid words'. Osborne's play is by no means free of the slang and topical minutiae which have caused Galsworthy's dialogue to wear so badly, and his wit is often the brittle, theatrical kind which has still less chance of standing up to time. But these flaws do not conceal the genuine rhetorical force which sustains Jimmy Porter's long speeches: they are at the same time violent and controlled, sardonically humorous and in deadly earnest, evoking occasional echoes of both Shaw and Strindberg.

Although so many of these impressive tirades are concerned

with the debased values of modern life, the action of the play is only very indirectly affected by such social questions as the class system. Alison describes Jimmy's invasion of her upper-class world as part of the class war he is still waging, with his wife as a hostage. His irritation over the absurdities of the English caste system does of course colour his whole view of life and enters into the frustrations of his marriage. But what he feels himself to be up against is not simply a class system but something less assailable and more frightening, a kind of intellectual inertia which cuts right across class distinctions, affecting the common Cliff as much as the well-bred Alison.

He is enraged by the lack of imaginative response he meets everywhere. 'Did you read Priestley's piece this week?', he asks Alison and Cliff. 'Why on earth I ask I don't know. I know damned well you haven't. Why do I spend ninepence on that damned paper every week? Nobody reads it except me. Nobody can be bothered. No one can raise themselves out of their delicious sloth. You two will drive me round the bend soon – I know it, as sure as I'm sitting here. I know you're going to drive me mad. Oh, heavens, how I long for a little ordinary human enthusiasm. Just enthusiasm – that's all. I want to hear a warm, thrilling voice cry out Hallelujah! Hallelujah! I'm alive! I've an idea. Why don't we have a little game? Let's pretend that we're human beings, and that we're actually alive. Just for a while. What do you say? Let's pretend we're human. Oh, brother, it's such a long time since I was with anyone who got enthusiastic about anything.'

Jimmy's anger has deep roots. He is one 'to whom the miseries of the world are misery, and will not let him rest'. He is capable of vicarious suffering, of living in other people's lives. He suffers for Hugh's mother, an old woman 'going through the sordid process of dying' just as he had suffered when a boy at the bedside of his dying father. This was his initiation into suffering: he recalls it for the benefit of Helena and Alison: 'Every time I sat on the edge of his bed, to listen to him talking or reading to me, I had to fight back my tears. At the end of twelve months, I was a veteran. All that feverish failure of a man had to listen to him was a small, frightened boy. I spent hour upon hour in that tiny bedroom. He would talk to me for hours, pouring out all that was left of his life to one lonely, bewildered little boy, who could barely understand half of what he said. All he could feel was the despair and the bitterness, the sweet, sickly smell of a dying man. You see, I learnt at an early age what it was to be angry – angry and helpless. And I can never forget it.'

Imaginative suffering is a profoundly solitary experience and Jimmy knows it. 'The heaviest, strongest, creatures in this world seem to be the loneliest,' he says to Alison. 'Like the old bear, following his own breath in the dark forest. There's no warm pack, no herd to comfort him. The voice that cries out doesn't have to be a weakling's, does it?' Alison is speaking ironically when she says, 'Don't take his suffering away from him. He'd be lost without it.' But the statement is true. Jimmy would be lost without it, yet at the same time, and very naturally, he resents the tormenting capacity with which he has been endowed. He kicks against the pricks, seeing all round him people who live their lives free of 'daemons', the 'untroubled', as O'Neill, another creator of haunted heroes, called them. 'They all want to escape from the pain of being alive,' he says, and longs for Alison to be initiated, to have a child that dies – 'Let it grow, let a recognisable human face emerge from that little mass of india rubber and wrinkles'. Such outbursts, on the verge of hysteria, indicate the strain which his sense of difference is placing on him. Alison makes communication between them finally impossible by withdrawing behind a façade of detached indifference. 'That girl there can twist your arm off with her silence', is Jimmy's bitter comment on her reaction. Her behaviour is also, of course, natural in the circumstances; they are both defeated by an incompatibility that goes too deep to be cured by sexual harmony.

Like so many of Strindberg's characters, Jimmy seeks from women far more than he could ever hope to get from them, and when he is disappointed turns on them with savage resentment. Release from his tormenting consciousness is what he is after. Alison had seemed to offer him this when he first fell in love with her. He was drawn to her by what seemed her 'wonderful relaxation of spirit'. But, as he puts it, 'In order to relax, you've first got to sweat your guts out', and this, as he soon discovers, is an experience Alison has never had. Her calm is only that of a Sleeping Beauty. His rage when he finds his mistake is irrational and unfair, yet at the same time, because it springs from so deep a need, it compels pity.

There is often an overtly wistful note in his attacks on people who have escaped 'the pain of being alive', by living in dreams or in the past. The Edwardian world evoked by Elgar is such a dream world: 'What a romantic picture. Phoney too, of course. It must have rained sometimes. Still, even I regret it somehow, phoney or not. If you've no world of your own, it's rather pleasant to regret the passing of someone else's.'

Sexual passion, which offers Jimmy an intermittent escape, cannot solve his problems. He alternates between sexual longing and loathing in a way that seems incomprehensible to the on-lookers in the play.

Why, why, why, why do we let these women bleed us to death? Have you ever had a letter, and on it is franked 'Please Give Your Blood Generously'? Well, the Postmaster-General does that, on behalf of all the women of the world. I suppose people of our generation aren't able to die for good causes any longer. We had all that done for us, in the thirties and the forties, when we were still kids. There aren't any good, brave causes left. If the big bang does come, and we all get killed off, it won't be in aid of the old-fashioned, grand design. It'll just be for the Brave New-nothing-very-much-thank-you. About as pointless and inglorious as stepping in front of a bus. No, there's nothing left for it, me boy, but to let yourself be butchered by the women.

The lament about missing causes in this passage is not meant to set us thinking of the good brave causes that *do* exist. This is not a play about causes but about a special kind of feeling, what Osborne has described as 'the texture of ordinary despair'.[3] Jimmy is a suffering hero, and the action is designed to illuminate his suffering rather than to force a conflict.

In a play written earlier, in collaboration with Anthony Creighton, *Epitaph for George Dillon* (11 February 1958, Royal

Court Theatre), the 'texture of ordinary despair' is again the staple of the play. George Dillon, actor and would-be playwright, feels himself to exist, like Jimmy Porter, in a different world from most people he meets. With Blake, these heroes cry, 'O why was I born with a different face?' He has quick perceptions – 'I have a mind and feelings that are all fingertips', is how he puts it. But he chooses to live with, and on, a suburban family who exist at an imaginative level well below the mediocre. Their feelings, in George Dillon's piquant metaphor, are: 'All thumbs, thumbs that are fat and squashy – like bananas, in fact, and rather sickly.'

The one intellectually sophisticated member of the family, Ruth, forces George to explore the reasons for his voluntary self-immolation among the Philistines. She gets beyond the superficial explanation, that he is a work-shy sponger, making capital out of a flaunted artistic temperament. Living with the Elliotts is not just an expedient for Dillon but a temptation. Among people who never ask questions he may stop asking himself tormenting questions about the nature of his talent: among people without imagination, he can give his own a rest.

Whether George has genuine talent or not is never shown, and is, in a sense, irrelevant. He certainly has the 'symptoms' and these alone prove too much for him. Talent, in Osborne's world, is a heavy burden, not to be taken on lightly. It is too heavy for George Dillon. He capitulates to the Philistines at the very moment when he is given some proof that his talent exists. He sells his 'dirtied up' play to make money on a provincial circuit and abdicates from all the responsibilities he would have to shoulder if he really were 'that mysterious, ridiculous being called an artist'. He succumbs first to tuberculosis and finally to the 'euthanasia' offered by marriage to the vacuous Josie. A weaker character than Jimmy Porter, he shrinks from the suffering that comes when the imagination is fully awake.

In the next play, *The Entertainer* (10 April 1957, Royal Court Theatre), Osborne studies the feeling of despair in a more advanced phase. Again, as in *Epitaph for George Dillon*, the central character is an artist, but this time a middle-aged one, Archie Rice, music-hall entertainer in a decaying music-hall.

Archie has passed to a stage beyond anger; that relief is only permitted to the younger generation in this play. His form of self-protection is an ironic detachment, a 'comedian's technique that absolves him from seeming committed to anyone or anything'. He tells Jean that he has stopped feeling – 'I don't give a damn about anything, not even women or draught Bass'. When he tells the 'worst, unfunniest stories in the world to a great mob of dead, drab erks', it doesn't matter, because 'I'm dead behind these eyes, I'm dead, just like the whole inert, shoddy lot out there'. His music-hall songs and patter reinforce this theme – 'Why should I care? Why should I let it touch me! . . . What's the use of despair, if they call you a square? . . . So why should I bother to care?'

Archie's bitterness about his relationship with his audience is in fact the proof of how much he is still feeling. For all his cynicism and general unscrupulousness, this seedy artist is a visionary: he has had to accept the second-rate, but he is not reconciled to it. He is haunted by memories of what the music hall had once been: they crystallise in the living figure of his father, Billie Rice, the 'One and Only'. The squalor and miseries of his life lie in the shadow of a revelation he experienced years before in an American bar, when he heard a negress singing a blues. He has never forgotten this intimation of what the human spirit was capable of expressing in art; he describes it to Jean:

But if ever I saw any hope or strength in the human race, it was in the face of that old fat negress getting up to sing about Jesus or something like that. She was poor and lonely and oppressed like nobody you've ever known. Or me, for that matter. I never even liked that kind of music, but to see that old black whore singing her heart out to the whole world, you knew somehow in your heart that it didn't matter how much you kick people, the real people, how much you despise them, if they can stand up and make a pure, just natural noise like that, there's nothing wrong with them, only with everybody else. I've never heard anything like that since. I've never heard it here. Oh, I've heard whispers of it on a Saturday night somewhere. Oh, he's heard it. Billy's heard it. He's heard them singing. Years ago, poor old gubbins. But you won't hear it anywhere now. I don't suppose we'll ever hear it again. There's nobody who can feel like that. I wish to God I could. I wish to God I could feel like that old black bitch with her fat cheeks, and sing. If I'd done one thing as good as that in my whole life, I'd have been all right.

The suffering from which George Dillon ran away is clearly shown here to be the necessary stuff of the artist's achievement. Archie grasps at his vision only once in the play, and it is at the moment of greatest suffering, when he learns that his young soldier son has been murdered by his kidnappers in Egypt. He says nothing at all, but slowly sings a blues, forcing his feeling to express itself in art.

The communication of feeling is presented in a more complex form in this play. Archie's bitterness over his failure to communicate artistically is shown to affect, and in its turn to be affected by, his failure in his private life. Like Osborne's other heroes, he is involved with women incapable of responding to his needs. Phoebe, his wife, is the sort of woman who cannot sit still and listen; she has to go to films she has forgotten before she comes home – '. . . you've got to go somewhere, as I say to him. You get bored stiff just sitting indoors.' But Osborne takes a great step forward in this play. There is no element of caricature about Phoebe, nor is she colourless. She is at once irritating and sympathetic, moving in her stoical acceptance of the harsh facts of her life, her fears of getting old and 'ending up in a long box in somebody else's front room in Gateshead, or was it West Hartlepool?' We can well understand why Archie wants to leave her, but we can also understand how a mutual tenderness has survived all the infidelities of their married life. It is she who waits for him on the stage at the end of the play, to hand him his hat and coat: this 'failure' is shown to have its own value.

The most complex and ambiguous relationship in the play is that between Archie and his daughter, Jean. Here the distribution of sympathy is equivocal. Jean, like Jimmy Porter, is harsh in her criticism of people who try to escape the pain of life – 'You're like everybody else,' she tells Archie, 'but you're worse – you think you can cover yourself by simply not bothering.' Jean is saddled with an unsuitable fiancé who appears at the end of the play for the sole purpose of being given his dismissal. He represents the 'untroubled' or, as Osborne puts it, the 'well-dressed, assured, well-educated people' whose 'emotional and imaginative capacity . . . is practically negligible'. The tragic events of the play, Billie's death, the killing of Mick, bring home to Jean the primary importance of right feeling: she expresses her need for it by breaking with her fiancé.

So far she and her father are in sympathy, since Archie, beneath his professional mask, is indubitably a man of feeling. But they part company on their ideas of how feeling should be expressed. Jean is a revolutionary in the Shavian tradition: like St Joan, only less effectively, she wants to change the world. Unlike St Joan, she has no faith in anything but man. 'Here we are,' she says, 'we're alone in the universe, there's no God, it just seems that it all began by something as simple as sunlight striking on a piece of rock. And here we are. We've only got ourselves. Somehow, we've just got to make a go of it.' Her attendance at a rally in Trafalgar Square is, to both her and Archie, a symbol of her philosophy: reason and good works, the betterment of the social conditions, these come first for her.

Archie is sceptical. He believes in her feeling in spite of, not because of 'all that Trafalgar Square stuff'. 'You're what they call a sentimentalist,' he tells her. 'You carry all your responses about with you, instead of leaving them at home. While everyone else is sitting on their hands you're the Joe at the back cheering and making his hands hurt. But you'll have to sit on your hands like everyone else.' To Archie, Jean's assumptions are arrogant. 'I still have a little dried pea of humility rattling around inside me,' he tells her. 'I don't think you have.' The 'little dried pea of humility' is the fruit of his travail as an artist: this 'failure' too has produced something of value.

With this play, for the first time, Osborne's drama became 'experimental' in the technical sense. He handles theatrical illusion with a new imaginative originality, achieving striking effects by alternating interior scenes with 'turns' on Archie's music-hall stage. There are some similarities to Brecht's method, but whereas Brecht was trying to stimulate detached thinking, Osborne is after greater emotional depth. 'I want to make people feel, to give them lessons in feeling,' he has said, 'The thinking can come afterwards.'⁴ The method helps him, as he says in his introductory note, to 'solve some of the eternal problems of time and space that face the dramatist.' We, the audience, are drawn into the heart of the play by this device. We are made to feel, by direct contact, what it means to be Archie Rice, the entertainer; we are in a better position to understand his bitterness.

We come to feel, too, an uneasy consciousness of the debased values this theatre supports. It is we, after all, the audience in the theatre within the theatre, who are sitting there, supposedly waiting for the nudes and getting the point of Archie's lewd innuendoes. After experiencing it for ourselves, we know what Osborne means when he says, 'The music hall is dying, and with it a significant part of England. Some of the heart of England has gone; something that once belonged to everyone, for this was truly a folk art.'

The music-hall image carries easily the theme of a degraded culture. It is also meant to convey something about the state of England, and this it does, though perhaps less forcefully. Yet the point is well made in certain scenes, when Archie, suffering himself from the results of political action, points the cynicism behind the patriotic jingles he sings. The two themes are brought together in the closing scene; Archie indicates the figure of Britannia, against the background of a nude tableau – 'I reckon she's sagging a bit, if you ask me' – and warns his audience, 'Don't clap too hard, we're all in a very old building.'

The implications of the theatre image reach even farther than this, however: in the closing moments they take on a Shakespearian rather than a Brechtian quality. The social themes drop away, leaving us with a final impression of man as a solitary being, the artist, dependent in the long run on some mysterious power that defies analysis. Archie's long story about the little man who insists on being natural even in Paradise brings the dramatic emphasis to bear on the strangeness of the human condition. It is with a 'mystery' that the play ends, as the shabby entertainer stands on the old, old stage 'in a little round world of light', telling jokes against Heaven while the 'man with the hook' waits in the wings. The entertainer's part is nearly over, but we, the audience, still have ours to play. 'Let me know where you're working tomorrow night', he says, 'and I'll come and see you.' Then the time comes for him to go, 'the little world of light snaps out, the stage is bare and dark. Archie Rice has gone.'

This is a superbly theatrical moment, rich in implications which are sensed intermittently throughout the play, and here brought together. Unquestionably the 'larger poetic imagination' is at work in such a scene, using resources which belong only to the theatre to create images that reach out far beyond it.

After such an imaginative outpouring, it was not surprising that Osborne should have needed to work at a lower tension in his next piece, *The World of Paul Slickey* (14 April 1959, The Pavilion, Bournemouth). Social questions are here in the fore-ground: the objects of Jimmy Porter's and Archie Rice's dislike are paraded and satirised in a lively, caustic, but somewhat disorganised entertainment, lacking the unifying element of feeling. Jack Oakham, the gossip columnist of *The Daily Racket* is in a situation that recalls *The Entertainer*: he purveys entertain-ment to suit the debased tastes he despises. His hard-bitten wife, Leslie, says of him: 'Jack has always suffered from excessive aspiration. There is a constant stain of endeavour underneath his emotional armpits. It throws off quite an unpleasant smell of sour ideals.'

In this description there is already a foretaste of *Luther* (26 June 1961, Theatre Royal, Nottingham). The 'excessive aspiration' which imperfectly motivates earlier characters becomes a main driving force in the hero of Osborne's most recent play. The historical character of Luther required very little adapting to be ideal for Osborne's characteristic dramatic purposes. He had to a high degree that capacity for suffering which was to him, as it is to Osborne, a sign of the elect. Some of the most striking passages in the play convey the sense of despair and panic that possessed Luther in his monastic life –

'I'm afraid of the darkness, and the hole in it, and I see it some time of every day! And some days more than once even, and there's no bottom to it, no bottom to my breath, and I can't reach it.'

The violence and rudeness of the historical Luther must also have endeared him to Osborne: it was the rudeness of a man impatient of conventional forms, a man of poetic temper, whose language burned with imaginative life: when he described something he took to be evil he made it sound evil, yielding no telling phrase, however gross, to the dictates of good taste. To the creator of Jimmy Porter and Archie Rice such a character was easy of imaginative realisation.

Jimmy Porter had asked, 'The voice that cries out doesn't have to be a weakling's, does it?' In *Luther* it sometimes seems that it is so. Dramatic emphasis is strongly laid on those aspects of his life that point to a state of neurotic anxiety: the key relationship with his father, the image of the lost child, prominent at the beginning and the end, the physical disabilities, especially the sweating and the constipation. Indeed, the constant reference to locked bowels conveys well the sense of a character locked up in his own tension and fear. In an essay of some years before,[5] Osborne had played with the idea that the 'prize neurotic' need not necessarily be revealed by introspective, withdrawn behaviour: the intense productive activity of apparently normal people might be serving as an outlet for 'deep-rooted anal preoccupations'. If this were true, Luther's public activities in the second, 'blaspheming' part of the play could be interpreted in terms of neurotic symptoms quite as well as his evident self-torturing in the first 'praising' part.

Osborne concludes, however, that this kind of analysis reduces history to the spectacle of Napoleons and Lenins 'busily staring down the lavatory pan'. This does not suggest that he would have decided to simplify Luther's story along such lines. The psychological factors are given their place – but they are not put forward as accounting for all that Luther was. His terrible sense of insecurity can be seen as stemming from an unsatisfactory filial relationship, but it is also true, as he is made to emphasise in his sermon, that life is insecure for everybody, and that every imaginative person must feel this: it is part of the human condition.

The dramatic emphasis rests on the question of faith, historically the central issue, as, in a different aspect, it is for our time. Osborne does no violence to history in dwelling on the struggle for, rather than the achievement of, faith. The historical Luther, who said that despair had once reduced him to wishing that he had never been created a man, provides the playwright with reasonable grounds for dramatising him as, above all, a man tormented by doubt. This aspect of Luther is well described in Cajetan's phrase: 'a man struggling for certainty, struggling insanely like a man in a fit, an animal trapped to the bone with doubt'. Luther himself admits to Staupitz in the final scene that he has never experienced certainty, even in his heroic moment at Worms. 'I listened for God's voice', he says, 'but all I could hear was my own.' The play shows him trying the 'three ways out of despair' he describes to Staupitz – 'One is faith in Christ, the second is to become enraged by the world and make its nose bleed for it, and the third is the love of a woman'. At the very end of the play he is still calling on his wife to drag him out of despair, the 'devil's own sweat'. He never arrives at any certainty except his certainty that God should be put back where He belongs, 'In each man's soul'.

Luther is the first of Osborne's heroes to be shown in conflict with his intellectual equals. His own views and those of the opposition, notably Cajetan and the Knight, are presented with equal dramatic plausibility, sometimes bringing to mind the celebrated justice of the trial scene in Shaw's *Saint Joan*. Cajetan, like Shaw's Inquisitor, makes a strong case for the authority of the Church; he sees Protestantism leading to the evils of nationalism and social unrest which are later demonstrated on the stage by a symbolic presentation of the peasants' rising and massacre. These are arguments, in fact, which have to be taken seriously. So do those of Staupitz who represents the real good that could exist in the monastic life: he is in many ways the most sympathetic character in the play. Osborne does not make the mistake of reducing Luther's stature by showing him in conflict with Aunt Sallies. Such obvious abuses as Tetzel's selling of indulgences are not allowed to call forth his worst anger; he uses them as a springboard to attack the whole idea of 'work holiness', proclaiming in its place his cardinal doctrine, 'The just shall live by faith'.

The most formidable adversaries he comes up against are his own father and the Knight. They both force on him an idea from which he shrinks: 'do you know what most men believe in their hearts – because they don't see in images like you do – they believe in their hearts that Christ was a man as we are'. When Luther maintains the power of the 'Word' the Knight dismisses it as 'poetry' – 'Why, none of it might be any more than poetry, have you thought of that, Martin?' Luther finds no answer to refute him: the dead body of the peasant lying between them seems indeed to discredit his religion. The Knight and Luther's father take their stand along with Jean in *The Entertainer* and Holyoake in Osborne's television play, *A Subject of Scandal and Concern.* They believe in 'our obligation to men': as Holyoake puts it, 'Are we not too poor to have God?'

Luther can take neither way: unable to accept that man is all, insisting on the power of God in the 'Word', he is also unable to accept the consolations of organised religion. Luther's God is 'utterly incomprehensible and beyond the reach of minds'. To the Knight this is tantamount to saying He does not exist: to Luther it means that He can only be reached by faith. The tension between the points of view is maintained to the end of the play, slackening only in the last scene, when Luther, holding his sleeping son in his arms, contemplates the mystery of faith and hope.

Osborne demonstrates in this play that he can command a fast-moving episodic form with as much ease as a restricted realistic one. The striking settings are presented as part of the whole imaginative effect; stage directions indicate an Expressionistic conception of certain scenes, such as Act 1, Scene 2, when Luther comes out of a cone surrounded by darkness, above him a great knife approaching the naked torso of a man. Osborne's rhetorical powers are put to good use in such a framework. He holds the stage with powerful scenes which are simply monologues, such as Tetzel's oration, Luther's sermon.

The virtuosity of these scenes, the skilful structure of the soliloquies, the ease with which Luther's recorded sayings blend into the dialogue, all witness to a dramatic eloquence rare in the theatre of today. *Luther* marks a new phase in Osborne's dramatic art. Its increased range and flexibility suggest interesting possibilities for his future development.

NOTES

1. Introduction to Lillah McCarthy, *Myself and Some Friends* (1933) reprinted in *Shaw on Theatre*, ed. J. West (1958) p. 217.

2. 'The Problem Play – a Symposium', in *The Humanitarian*, VI (May 1895). In *Shaw on Theatre*, p. 63.

3. John Osborne, 'They call it Cricket', in *Declaration*, ed. Tom Maschler (1957) p. 69.

4. *Declaration*, p. 65.

5. *Declaration*, p. 72.

George E. Wellwarth

JOHN OSBORNE: 'ANGRY YOUNG MAN'? (1964)

THE 'new movement' in the British drama actually began officially on the night of May 8, 1956, when John Osborne's *Look Back in Anger* opened at the Royal Court Theatre in London. The reviews in the daily newspapers the next day were in general cautiously favorable. But it was not until Kenneth Tynan's review came out the following Sunday that the 'movement' was properly launched. Tynan climaxed his panegyric by saying, 'I agree that *Look Back in Anger* is likely to remain a minority taste. What matters, however, is the size of the minority. I estimate it at roughly 6,733,000, which is the number of people in this country between the ages of twenty and thirty. And this figure will doubtless be swelled by refugees from other age-groups who are curious to know precisely what the contemporary young pup is thinking and feeling. I doubt I could love anyone who did not wish to see *Look Back in Anger*. It is the best young play of its decade.'[1] This will strike most people as pretentious, self-publicizing gush rather than criticism, but it had its effect. Overnight, Osborne, previously an obscure provincial actor, became famous; and sundry despairing young playwrights who had been furtively scribbling away in seedy rooming houses on the Earl's Court Road, in Hampstead, Hackney, Poplar, Whitechapel, and Newington Butts suddenly took heart and set to with renewed industry. They were fortunate. John Osborne's timing was precisely right. A few years earlier or a few years later *Look Back in Anger* might well have been passed off by the critics as callow breast-beating, but in 1956 the critics and the public were ready for something new. The sincerity of the Osborne play must have come as a tremendous relief after the seemingly endless stream of elephantiasis-afflicted plots trying to be fey that characterized the efforts of the fashionable West End dramatists. There was also the factor of the international success of Arthur Miller and Tennessee Williams. At last some-one had appeared who could challenge the Americans' position as representatives of the English-speaking drama. Chauvinism stirred in the critics as they watched *Look Back in Anger*; and the angry-young-man movement was born. Now, one play doth not a movement make; hence the renewed scraping of pens in Earl's Court and Hackney The new English playwrights got their chance because English national pride was aroused by the success of Osborne's first play.

Look Back in Anger was a rallying point. It came to represent the dissatisfaction with society reflected in the novels of such young writers as John Wain, Kingsley Amis, and John Braine. Jimmy Porter, its rancorous protagonist, was thought to symbolize the fury of the young postwar generation that felt itself betrayed, sold out, and irrevocably ruined by its elders.[2] The older generation had made a thorough mess of things, and there was nothing the new generation could do except withdraw (Jimmy Porter, an educated and cultured university graduate, supports himself by peddling candy in the streets) and indulge in the perverse and vicarious pleasure of nursing its resentment. Society is so rotten that there is no longer any point in attempting to be useful. It is not that Jimmy is *content* to stagnate. He just feels that he has no chance. His withdrawal is not one of choice. He does not even permit himself the consolation of gloating over conditions with the cynical hindsight of superiority. He simply feels himself to be unjustly crushed down with no visible hope of ever getting up again. He reminds one of a fighter who has been knocked down, and, instead of getting up again, just lies there spitting insults at his opponent and grinning with sardonic masochism whenever the latter kicks him in the ribs.

But is this what Osborne really intended when he wrote the play? Or has it been read into it by eager critics who have been searching for a symbol of a new postwar 'lost generation' to rival Hemingway's creation of Jake Barnes as a personification of post-World War I disillusionment? Is Jimmy's defeatism a symbol of the numb quiescence of post-World War II youth, as Jake's castration was of the sterile euphoria of post-World War I youth?

John Osborne must have been the most surprised man in England when he suddenly found himself placed at the head of the angry-young-man movement.[3] He had written a carefully and intelligently worked out dramatic study of a psychotic marriage relationship and was hailed instead as the creator of a revolutionary literary movement. Certainly Jimmy Porter makes a good many cutting remarks about contemporary society, but he only makes them as a result of his own peculiar personality problems. There is absolutely no indication in the play that Osborne ever intended Jimmy's remarks to be taken as a general condemnation of society. Jimmy is an extremely unusual young man and anything but representative of the young men of our time. Osborne has not put his diatribes against society in his mouth in order to orate in the manner of a Hyde Park soap-box messiah. Instead, Jimmy's rantings are always the natural outgrowth of his psychotic state: they are a defense mechanism he uses to hurt his wife, whom he suspects of being imperfectly devoted to him, and to avoid facing up to the problem of his own helpless character. Granted that a representative of the generation which reached adulthood in the early fifties would execrate his elders (what generation this side of early Victorianism has not?), his anger could hardly be embodied in Jimmy's rantings if any justice is to be done to him. He has a right to rant and he has a right to be heard; he has a right even to throw up his hands in disgust and retire, whether it be into a Zen or a beatnick euphoria or simply into a flabby, unthinking, irresponsible lassitude. But Jimmy's tirades are not representative of any attitude. Osborne has given Jimmy a certain facility in composing biting remarks, but there is no real sense, no mature criticism in those remarks. Examined closely, Jimmy Porter's self-conscious orations are the veritablest sophomoric piffle.

Look Back in Anger was strenuously fiddled up into an epoch-making play by the London critics. It is nothing of the sort; but, on the other hand, it is by no means a worthless play either.

Osborne has created an excellent, minutely accurate dissection of a perverse marriage in the style of Strindberg. *Look Back in Anger* irresistibly recalls the Swedish author's *Dance of Death*. Jimmy Porter's problem is not the vicious injustice and hypocrisy of the social order: it is his suppressed awareness of the insoluble psychological paradox caused by his desperate, overriding need to possess a woman's complete, unquestioning love and his simultaneous constitutional inability to get along with anyone. His outbursts are the overflow of his bitterness whenever his wife fails to measure up to the standards of devotion that he expects of her at the same time that he knows them to be impossible. Jimmy's biting sarcasms are in a sense really directed inwardly against himself in the manner of the guilt-ridden Dostoyevskian hero who tortures himself by torturing others. His real purpose, as he deliberately tries to destroy his wife's love for him because it is not the love he had envisioned, is self-laceration. Jimmy is the sort of man who needs, but is too proud to demand, absolute devotion. He needs it all the more from Alison because she comes from the sort of upper-class family which he, as a good socialist, despises as useless and effete and which at the same time he envies and resents because he knows that it looks down on him. In order to possess her he has had to marry her and submit to the conventionality that he hates. His dilemma is perfectly presented in Alison's description of his reaction to her virginity: 'afterwards, he actually taunted me with my virginity. He was quite angry about it, as if I had deceived him in some strange way. He seemed to think that an untouched woman would defile him.'⁴ By being a virgin she is pulling him into the vortex of social convention. She is what she is *expected* to be in *her* circle. But Jimmy cannot show pleasure because that would be the conventional reaction, though if his wife were not virginal he would have to resent it as evidence of her fickleness. What he really wants, as Alison explains to her friend, Helena (who becomes Jimmy's mistress when Alison leaves him), is 'something quite different from us. What it is exactly I don't know – a kind of cross between a mother and a Greek courtesan, a henchwoman, a mixture of Cleopatra and

Boswell.'5 Jimmy's tragedy is simply that he will never find this ideal, and he knows it. He will spend the rest of his life bathed in self-pity, yammering impotently at the misfortunes he himself has created.

Osborne's second play, *The Entertainer* (1957), was a clumsily constructed hodgepodge about a talentless vaudeville actor with the morals and feelings of a toad. It is chiefly interesting as a first fumbling attempt at the Brechtian episodic method which Osborne used later in *Luther*.

Epitaph for George Dillon (1958) was actually Osborne's first play, written in collaboration with Anthony Creighton, but it was not produced until the success of *Look Back in Anger* had established Osborne's name as 'safe'. It deals with a lazy and basically untalented young man who is trying to become a playwright with a minimum of effort. Unable to get anyone interested in his laborious attempts at serious drama, he sells out to a producer of honky-tonk road shows, and then submerges himself completely in the bourgeois milieu that he despises by marrying the brainless daughter of the family that has been supporting him. Dillon is a heartless chiseler, but his fall is the fall of the artist who finds the inertia of society too much for him and just gives up.

Another interpretation that could be applied to the play is that it is about the fragility of artistic integrity. Dillon starts out by attempting to be a serious playwright. He tries to gain time and comfort by sponging off an ordinary, middle-class family. He amuses himself by playing the part of the great and enigmatic artist for their benefit and sniggering to himself whenever their backs are turned. But sooner or later his bluff has to be called, and he has to sell out to the honky-tonk promoter to save the image he has manufactured. Someone once said – it was Hemingway, I think – that an artist's integrity is like a woman's virginity: once lost it can never be regained. Dillon illustrates the truth of this perfectly. Once he has compromised himself he *has* to sell out and do hack work. Thus when the family swallows him up at the end, it seems natural and inevitable to us. The power of inner resistance can only be maintained by constant use, Osborne and Creighton are saying; George Dillon bends once and is lost.

By the time *Look Back in Anger* and *The Entertainer* were produced, Osborne had been hailed as the angry young man so much that he had actually become one. If there is a prototype of the angry-young-man play, *The World of Paul Slickey* is it. Written as a musical, it failed when first produced. And no wonder. There is so much direct criticism of society (castigation would perhaps be a better word) in it that just about everyone must have been made uncomfortable. When criticizing social institutions on the stage it is advisable to use the gentle touch if one wishes to have a successful show. People will accept the offhand slaps of a witty mind because if they can laugh at the object of the satire they can feel superior to it: nobody consciously identifies himself with ridiculousness. But even if they will allow themselves to be slapped under the illusion that someone else is being slapped, they will not allow themselves to be openly and directly attacked. Osborne is no George Dillon. He does not compromise. He does not slip unobtrusively under his opponent's guard: he beats it down with a two-fisted attack. He is an angry young man, not a contemptuous one. *The World of Paul Slickey* is pure spit and vomit thrown directly into the teeth of the audience. Commercially it has been Osborne's least successful play; artistically it is his best. Inability to compromise may be disastrous from a diplomatic viewpoint, but art is not diplomacy: it is truth.

In his dedication Osborne leaves no doubt as to his intentions:

No one has ever dedicated a string quartet to a donkey although books have been dedicated to critics. I dedicate this play to the liars and self-deceivers; to those who daily deal out treachery; to those who handle their professions as instruments of debasement; to those who, for a salary cheque and less, successfully betray my country; and those who will do it for no inducement at all. In this bleak time, when such men have never had it so good, this entertainment is dedicated to their boredom, their incomprehension, their distaste. It would be a sad error to raise a smile from them. A donkey with ears that could listen would no longer be a donkey; but the day may come when he is left behind because the other animals have learned to hear.[6]

During the play Osborne lashes out indiscriminately at, among other things, the cold war, the arms race, parliamentary double talk, scandalmongers, debased public taste, vindictive legal punishment (a character sings a song advocating a return to beheading because hanging is too crude), income-tax evasion by the rich, popular songs, and the prostitution act (get them off the streets: see no evil, hear no evil, speak no evil – just do it!). All these criticisms are embodied in the songs scattered throughout the work. The framework of the plot is directed against love as practised in the modern world, which Osborne sees as merely passionless lust.

It is a pity that the intensity and frankness of the anger in *The World of Paul Slickey* will always prevent its being popular, for it is a good play. In it Osborne finally becomes the angry young man.

In *A Subject of Scandal and Concern* (1960) and *Luther* (1961), Osborne continues to be the angry young man, but he seems to have absorbed the lesson of *The World of Paul Slickey*. In these two plays Osborne attacks the establishment indirectly instead of leaving his glove in its face. Both plays concern historical characters, and Osborne leaves the implication very clear for us that 'it could happen again'.

Despite the fact that the play is about a trial that took place in 1842, the very title, *A Subject of Scandal and Concern*, indicates Osborne's sense of the immediacy and urgency of the problem. This short television play is about the trial of George Jacob Holyoake, who was the last person tried for the 'crime' of blasphemy in England. Holyoake's offense consisted in stating publicly that he did not believe in God and that the amount of money spent on religion was criminally large in view of the fact that a great many people were living in a poverty which could be substantially relieved by the diversion of church funds to charitable purposes. Curiously enough, although George Holyoake was the last person actually to be imprisoned in

England for the 'crime' of blasphemy, it would still be dangerous from a social and professional standpoint, if not from a legal one, for a man in a responsible public position (Holyoake was a teacher) openly to proclaim his atheism. That, of course, is the point over which Osborne is exercised. He gets it across by having a modern lawyer serve as narrator to the play. He treats the action patronizingly, as befits a modern lawyer talking about an archaic legal problem, but at the end of the play it becomes evident that the lawyer, who has been sitting in a prison interview room, is about to represent a client in a case similar to Holyoake's.

Luther presents a more difficult problem. Written in an imitation of Brecht's epic style, it presents a series of historically accurate episodes from Luther's career. Osborne takes Luther from the time he is admitted into the Augustinian Order in 1506 to his declining years, when he is living with his wife and child in the now abandoned convent in which he celebrated his first mass. At the beginning of each scene a knight carrying a banner appears and 'Briefly barks the time and place of the scene following at the audience'.[7]

Osborne's main purpose in *Luther* is to continue in a less offensive way the angry young man literature expected of him. *The World of Paul Slickey* was unpalatable because an audience likes to identify with at least one of the characters in a play – but the world of Paul Slickey was inhabited by uniformly despicable characters. The only angry young man in that play was outside it – John Osborne in person, dribbling black bile and trying to spatter the audience with it. In *Luther*, however, the angry young man is the hero, and the audience can easily identify with this hero – a universally respected religious reformer dead over three hundred years.

There is no harm at all in identifying with such a man and in feeling indignation with him at society. It is easy to feel rebellious and indignant when society is represented by such as John Tetzel. We all notice that Tetzel is nothing but a Madison Avenue or Tottenham Court Road huckster, but the effort to transpose him is too much. He remains a sixteenth century figure – painless and harmless. In short, *Luther* is the sort of thing that might and should have been written during the second World War if England had been occupied by the Nazis. Anouilh's *Antigone* would not have been acclaimed as a very effective play if it had been produced in 1961 either. It must be said in Osborne's defense, however, that when he did write a completely honest play – *The World of Paul Slickey* – the public reacted as if their seats were fitted with slowly emerging spikes.

As long as Osborne sticks to his point, emasculated as it necessarily is by the transposition of time and place and by the inevitable intrusion of purely religious considerations, he does well. The scene in which Tetzel gives his sales oration is first-class writing and first-class drama. But this scene and one other are the only ones in which Osborne is able to make a point. The other scene is the one showing Luther's dispute with Johan von Eck at the Diet of Worms, in which Eck makes the now all too familiar plea that we must stick together and that anyone who thinks differently or questions the *status quo* is an enemy since he gives the real enemy the impression that there is dissension and, consequently, dissatisfaction. Besides this there is nothing but pretentious, overblown rhetoric – Osborne simply lacks a poetic style – and sloppy symbolism. Osborne's repeated references to Luther's constipation may lead the spectator to believe that he attributes the rise of the Reformation to the constant exacerbation of Luther's mind and spirit by the stubborn flabbiness of his lower intestine – a theory which I would be the last to reject. Who knows what world-shaking events are really ultimately traceable to some great man's irritation with the chambermaid's lack of complacency or with the inordinate activity of the fleas in his wig? Osborne's theory is surely a valid one – but what is one to do with an author who can write lines like these: 'I'm like a ripe stool in the world's straining anus, and at any moment we're about to let each other go'?[8]

Since *Luther*, Osborne has written two short plays, *The Blood of the Bambergs* and *Under Plain Cover*, produced together at the Royal Court Theatre in July, 1962, under the collective title of *Plays for England*. They reveal only too clearly what one is to do with him – leave him unproduced. That these two plays were accepted by a professional management is in itself incredible, and is a disturbing indication of how far the directors of the Royal Court have become bemused by the mirage of the 'movement' which they initiated and nursed along. *The Blood of the Bambergs* is so unbelievably bad, so monumentally inept, that it would have earned its author instant and deserved expulsion from any competently taught amateur playwriting class. *Under Plain Cover* illustrates the fact that Shaw's remark about the net result of the English stage censorship being to let through embarrassingly tasteless exhibitions while it bars serious discussions of sexual relationships is as true now as it was in the eighteen-nineties.

The genesis of these two plays is not difficult to reconstruct. What happened, probably, is that Osborne, feeling that it was time to write a new play, started casting about for fresh things to be angry at. He decided to be angry at (i) the phoniness and extravagances of royalty, and (ii) the prejudicial attitude which the bourgeoisie adopts toward people who amuse themselves with some of the gamier practices described by Krafft-Ebing.

The Blood of the Bambergs seems to have been vaguely inspired by the Anthony Armstrong-Jones–Princess Margaret wedding. At any rate, it involves the wedding of a photographer with royalty. The real bridegroom has been killed in a car crash while speeding to the ceremony. The preparations have been so elaborate and costly that the organizers do not dare call it off. They explain that the government will inevitably fall if the ceremony is not held and cast desperately about for a solution to their difficulty. They are about to give up in despair when (surprise! surprise!) they find, fast asleep in the deserted cathedral, an Australian photographer who is really an illegitimate son of the Prince of Bamberg and the dead prince's double. The rest of the play is merely a witless farrago of disorganized scenes, none of them germane to anything in real life.

The critics did not have anything good to say about *The Blood of the Bambergs*, but they were kinder to *Under Plain Cover*. Kenneth Tynan was the most enthusiastic, as usual. He found that 'Mr. Osborne's courage is doubly flabbergasting: not only does he state the facts about a sadomasochistic *ménage*, he also refrains from condemning it.' He goes on to say that 'perhaps the most audacious statement ever made on the English stage' is that 'an anal-sadistic relationship need not preclude love'.[9]

The second of the *Plays for England* is about a young married couple whose pleasure it is to dress up in various costumes and act out sadomasochistic sexual fantasies. Between charades they indulge themselves in lengthy and incredibly boring fetishistic discussions of female underwear. After a bit, a newspaper reporter ambles on and informs us that, unbeknownst to them, Tim and Jenny are really brother and sister. Parted as little children, they met and fell in love as grownups (by a coincidence no more or less contrived than the convenient discovery of a bastard Bamberg snoozing in the cathedral), married, had two children, and lived happily with their fetishes and their charades. Tim and Jenny are parted, and Jenny marries someone else. She then runs away and returns to Tim. For seven years they live together in their old house, never once going out and presumably parading happily around in their underwear. Then the reporter appears again, and gives us what is presumably Osborne's message: 'To Timothy and Jenny I leave this message. You can't escape the world. Even if you want to, it won't let you. Come out then, I say. Show yourselves. Be brave. Be courageous. Fear not. Fear not.'[10] Osborne seems to be suggesting here that sexual perverts should flaunt their abnormalities publicly – or at least that they should be permitted to do as they please. But the problem, surely, is that they find it necessary to do it. The immaturity of Osborne's thought processes can be seen by comparing *Under Plain Cover* to Pinter's *The Lover*, which deals with very much the same theme. Pinter's treatment is sophisticated, accurate, witty, and meaningful; Osborne's is jejune and tasteless. Instead of being a protest, *Under Plain Cover* is only the cheaply sensational story it purports to be protesting against.

It is doubtful that anything significant can be expected from John Osborne after *Plays for England*. He has become a victim of his own critical success. Left alone, he might have developed into a modestly talented writer of competently constructed, slightly acidulous hack plays. The strong streak of trite sentimentality which marred *Look Back in Anger* would undoubtedly have taken over had Osborne not been promoted into the figurehead of a new 'movement', and he would have peacefully joined the ranks of the television and provincial repertory company playwrights. Osborne is now committed to being angry; but he got all his anger off his chest in *The World of Paul Slickey*. In *Luther* he tackled a subject far beyond his intellectual powers. The result was ludicrous rather than enlightening. In *Plays for England* he is preaching – and making no more sense than if he were fulminating from a real pulpit.

NOTES

1. *The Observer*, 13 May 1956, p. 11.
2. J. Russell Taylor (*Anger and After* (1963) pp. 40–5) recognizes that *Look Back in Anger* is basically a well-made, domestic-psychological drama, but he spoils his analysis by desperately trying to twist it into an angry-young-man play with the aid of isolated passages taken out of context.
3. Osborne himself characterized *Look Back in Anger* as 'a formal, rather old-fashioned play', and said that he did not dare 'pick up a copy of *Look Back* nowadays. It embarrasses me.' (John Osborne, 'That Awful Museum,' *Twentieth Century*, CLXIX (Feb. 1961) 216.)
4. John Osborne, *Look Back in Anger* (New York, 1959) p. 28.
5. Ibid. p. 113.
6. John Osborne, *The World of Paul Slickey* (1959) p. [5].
7. John Osborne, *Luther* (New York, 1961) p. 11.
8. Ibid. p. 55.
9. *The Observer*, 22 July 1962, p. 20.
10. John Osborne, *Plays for England* (1963) pp. 135–6.

Geoffrey Carnall

SAINTS AND HUMAN BEINGS: ORWELL, OSBORNE AND GANDHI (1965)

NEAR the end of John Osborne's play *Look Back in Anger*, Jimmy Porter accuses Helena of wanting to escape from the pain of being alive – of wanting to escape from love. Helena has been living with him, but is now withdrawing in favour of Alison, Jimmy's lawful wife. She cannot, she says, bear taking part in all this suffering. Jimmy replies she'd better give up the whole idea of life, and become a saint: she'll never make it as a human being. Those who love need muscle and guts. It is not for people who cannot bear the thought of messing up their nice clean souls.[1]

The antithesis of saint and human being, with a preference for the human being, has a long history. But the immediate source of Jimmy Porter's use of the doctrine appears to have been an essay by George Orwell, on Gandhi. At least, Orwell prefers human beings to saints in words that sound like Jimmy's. The saint, says Orwell, wants to 'escape from the pain of living, and above all from love, which, sexual or non-sexual, is hard work'. Non-attachment, the ideal of the saint, is *easier* than attachment. To fasten one's love upon other human individuals means that one must be prepared to be 'defeated and broken up by life'.[2]

George Orwell was no doubt taking the idea more seriously than Mr Osborne. Jimmy Porter finds it a convenient form of attack on a well-bred young woman with a taste for churchgoing. But there is a sense in which it sums up the play. *Look Back in Anger* does make a virtue of willingness to be defeated and broken up; and the feeling of defeat is a genuine link between Jimmy Porter and George Orwell. Orwell not only took part in the Spanish Civil War on the losing side; he belonged to a faction on the losing side which was itself suppressed by its co-belligerents. Mr Osborne, for his part, forms his hero's character at the bedside of a dying victim of the same civil war. Jimmy early learnt what it was to be angry and helpless.

The helplessness is as distinctive as the anger. Much of the appeal originally made by the play clearly came from its driving, remorseless energy. But its deepest fascination comes from the association of this energy with a sense of futility. Energy usually needs a sense of effectiveness. *Look Back in Anger* contrives to dispense with the need. In an increasingly bewildering world, it is an achievement calculated to awaken a response in many people.

There is, of course, an element of effectiveness in the action of the play. Its momentum comes from the successful humiliation of Alison. Jimmy wants to see her face rubbed in the mud, and in the end she accepts her role as the dominated partner, grovelling, crawling: on which terms Jimmy is very willing to play the bear to her squirrel, in an uprush of tender affection. The significance of the game of bears and squirrels has already been explained by Alison. It was, she tells Helena, an escape into dumb, uncomplicated affection in a cosy zoo for two, 'a silly symphony for people who couldn't bear the pain of being human beings any longer'.[3] Human beings are seen being human when they accept the horror and futility of life. To be more precise, Jimmy exerts himself to draw Alison into a communion of the lost. He believes vehemently in the educational value of death-bed vigils, and wishes that Alison could have a child so that it could die: it might, he says, help her to become a recognisable human being.[4]

Mr Osborne's great achievement in this play is to give such vindictive energy a high-spirited declamatory expression which enables the audience to identify with Jimmy Porter and join in the act. Something of this destructive power forms part of the enduring appeal of George Orwell's work also. It is not that Orwell has Mr Osborne's exhilarating virtuosity – the ability to imagine Alison's mother bellowing like a rhinoceros in labour. On the contrary, the temper of his work is consistently lowering. It seems to be written, as he said of Swift, in a mood like that of someone suffering from jaundice or the after-effects of influenza.

But this depressed atmosphere is an admirable preparation for witheringly comprehensive attacks: seductively exhilarating in their very comprehensiveness.

In his essay on Donald McGill (of the comic postcards), Orwell suggests that there is a Don Quixote and a Sancho Panza in all of us. One part of us wishes to be a hero or a saint; another part is 'a little fat man who sees very clearly the advantages of staying alive with a whole skin'. The comic postcard is a fine statement of the Sancho Panza view of life – the view which no society can afford either to encourage or to ignore: although official literature does its best to ignore it. Orwell could never read this official literature – military proclamations, speeches by national leaders, solidarity songs, temperance tracts, papal encyclicals – 'without seeming to hear in the background a chorus of raspberries from all the millions of common men to whom these high sentiments make no appeal'. Few readers will fail, I suspect, to be elated by that chorus of raspberries; but Orwell is careful to deny one the satisfaction of supposing that it is an intimation of effective revolt. 'When it comes to the pinch, human beings are heroic.'[5] The authors of official literature will not have to worry.

Orwell has effectively deflated both official literature and rebellion against it. The rebellion is justified but ultimately pointless. It is this attitude which finds its most elaborate expression in *Animal Farm* and *1984*. The animals had good reason to expel Mr Jones, but the regime of the pigs is no improvement. Winston Smith is right to rebel against the totalitarian society of Oceania, but the rebellion leads nowhere. While the origin of this pessimism is partly to be found in the grim history of Europe in the 'thirties and 'forties, it was also the product of experiences much earlier in Orwell's life. One gets a hint of them in his essay on the preparatory school which he attended. When he first went there he was apt to wet his bed. In those days, bed-wetting was regarded as a disgusting crime, and in due course Orwell was beaten to deter him from committing it. He knew that bed-wetting was wicked. He also knew that it was outside his control. It was a sin that he did not want to commit, but could not avoid committing. He acquiesced in this profound injustice, and in fact stopped wetting his bed. Repeated beating was not only unjust; it was also effective. Orwell protests against the barbarity of the treatment, but the impression left by his narrative is less one of protest than of stoic endurance of what then seemed unquestionable powers, infecting him with a sense of inferiority, and 'the dread of offending against mysterious, terrible laws'.[6]

Orwell was probably uncertain to the last about how far the world really was governed by such laws. He did not want to think that it was, but this made him all the more cautious about rejecting the idea. As he observes in his 'Notes on Nationalism', if one's emotions are involved, grossly obvious but inconvenient facts are intolerable and must be denied.[7] He was dedicated to attacking totalitarianism and promoting democratic socialism, but he prided himself on his ability to insulate his subjective feelings from his thinking, and to 'make predictions cold-bloodedly, by the book of arithmetic'.[8] *1984* is one such prediction; and if he denies himself the satisfaction of portraying the defeat of tyranny, he gets some pleasure out of his sense of skill in using the book of arithmetic. So, incidentally, does the reader.

None the less, Orwell was unsure of the truth of his predictions. Although he was nagged by a belief in the probable defeat of the human spirit, a more hopeful note can sometimes be heard in his writings. His grimmer prophecies should not be viewed in isolation. He might assert, in 1942, that in our time, no one believes in any sanction greater than military power. 'There is no "law", there is only power.' He is not arguing that this is true, only that modern men do in fact think it true: those who deny this being intellectual cowards, or disguised power-worshippers, or people who had 'simply not caught up with the age they are living in'.[9] It is evident, however, that he had himself only just caught up with the age, because in the previous year he had noted with pleasure that the English still believed in the idea of impartial law. 'The totalitarian idea that there is no such thing as law, there is only power, has never taken root.'[10] He conceded that this belief might be an illusion, but it was a beneficent one.

I do not think this necessarily represents a firm development in his thinking between 1941 and 1942. A similar shifting of attitude can be observed during the post-war years in his assessment of the prospects of a free society. The atomic bomb made him fear the worst, because it was an expensive weapon and therefore specially convenient for tyrants. A state which possessed it would be at once unconquerable and in a permanent state of cold war with its neighbours. The result could be an epoch 'as horribly stable as the slave empires of antiquity'.[11] In his 'Second Thoughts on James Burnham' (1946), however, he rejected the notion of a huge, invincible, everlasting slave empire. Such an empire could not endure, because 'certain rules of conduct have to be observed if human society is to hold together at all'. The Soviet regime (he was writing, of course, in Stalin's time) 'will either democratise itself, or it will perish'.[12] Gloomier possibilities, however, obsessed his imagination. The difficult hope sketched in the essay on Burnham must have seemed fragile indeed when measured against the apparatus of modern tyranny. Yet one can see him speculating on the possibility of hope as late as the essay which he wrote after Gandhi's death. Admittedly he questioned whether the nature of modern totalitarianism was ever really understood by Gandhi, believing as he did that it was always possible for a popular leader to command publicity. Nevertheless, Orwell still admitted the possible relevance of Gandhi's faith that all people are more or less approachable. He questioned this belief, but thought it important. He doubted whether civilisation could stand another major war, 'and it is at least thinkable that the way out lies through non-violence'.[13]

The essay on Gandhi is moving because it renders so finely Orwell's uncertainty about his own destructive pessimism. It is obvious that Gandhi can readily be fitted into devastating Orwellian categories; the life-avoiding saint, the old-fashioned man who doesn't understand the world he is living in. But Orwell hesitates to dismiss him thus, because his campaigns did after all have a success that power-politicians would not have expected. He kept up the struggle against the British obstinately and without hatred. Compared to other politicians, Orwell concludes, 'how clean a smell he has managed to leave behind!'[14]

Orwell does not do much to analyse that clean smell, but it is evidently connected with an attitude to defeat radically different from his own. Gandhi had an unusual capacity for pursuing what seemed to him the right thing to do, independently of what others thought or did, and with relatively little anxiety about immediate results. The point could be illustrated in many ways, but it may be enough here to look at some advice he gave to British pacifists during the Second World War. He was commenting on an article by Dr Maude Royden, who had been told that if she could stop war with spiritual power, she should do it; and that if she couldn't, she should let others do what they could. 'And if you are right', her critic went on, 'in thinking that war is so damnable that anyone who takes part in it is damned, then I would rather be damned than let these things go on without doing all I can to stop them.'[15] This person obviously shared Jimmy Porter's distaste for those who can't bear the thought of messing up their nice clean souls.

What was Gandhi's reply? He said that pacifists should not lose faith because they produce no visible effect on the course of events. 'They should believe that their action will produce tangible results in due course', and live for 'the anti-war effort which is bound to succeed sooner rather than later, if man is to live as man and not become a two-footed brute'. Gandhi was willing to wait for the moment when 'fruitful expostulation' was possible, willing meanwhile to put up with the feeling of powerlessness, the feeling that his day was over. He could busy himself with constructive work in the villages, and show little concern with the thought that he might be finished as a political force. And even when murderous hatred between Hindus and Muslims engulfed whole provinces, and he felt himself to be in utter darkness, he still remained convinced that it was because he and others had not shown enough devotion to non-violence: it was no argument against non-violence itself.

Orwell might have found it easier to take Gandhi seriously if he had lived to see the development of a less monolithic communism after 1956. Gomulka's Poland is something that he might have found worth waiting for. As it is, the Gandhi essay, like the earlier essay on James Burnham, stands as a mere question-mark beside the remorselessly singleminded assurance of *1984*.

John Osborne, for his part, continues to feel most at home with those who have never made a decision that they didn't either regret, or suspect was just plain commonplace, or shifty, or scamped and indulgent, or stupid and undistinguished. But he too has a question-mark beside his sombre view of human nature: his play about Martin Luther.

Luther appears to have been inspired by a psycho-analytical study of the reformer by Erik H. Erikson: *Young Man Luther*. (The book was brought out by Mr Osborne's own publisher, Faber & Faber, in 1959.) Mr Osborne was bound to appreciate Dr Erikson's portrayal of Luther as one who did the dirty work of his age, a victim of the kind of crisis which makes neurotic patients out of people 'until they find a cure – and this often means a cause'.[16] In the perspective offered by Dr Erikson, it is possible to view Jimmy Porter's longing for a good brave cause, his unwillingness to commit himself to anything more absorbing than selling sweets in the market, as a condition necessary before a new identity, a new style of life, can be discovered. It is no adequate objection to say, as many have said of Jimmy, that he is merely a neurotic personality in a limited situation – 'a very tiresome young man', to quote Helena. Many of those who refuse to submit to an empty faith, a collective impotence, meaningless work, do not succeed in pushing beyond a bare refusal. But the refusal still has within it the possibility of creation: the creativity of a Luther – or a Hitler (Dr Erikson's book contains an illuminating analysis of Hitler as a young man).[17] And Martin Luther, confused and disappointing as his rebellion must appear to those who think like Mr Osborne, did undeniably create on a massive scale. To the objection of the papal legate that he was tearing down Christendom without knowing what to put in its place, Osborne's Luther replies, as Jimmy Porter might have done: 'A withered arm is best amputated, an infected place is best scoured out, and so you pray for healthy tissue and something sturdy and clean that was crumbling and full of filth.'[18]

Mr Osborne is not specially interested in Dr Erikson's interpretation of monastic life as a 'moratorium' in which the young man prepared himself for his as yet undiscovered vocation. It remains, in the play, a place of shelter for people who have 'given up': saints, in fact, not human beings. What Osborne is interested in is Luther's partial – only partial – liberation from the conflicts which contort his mind and constipate his bowels. His imagination is impressed by the moment on the cloaca when Luther attained knowledge that the just shall live by faith. Jimmy Porter stank: and that was all there was to it. Luther, in moments of crisis, breaks out into a stench that can be smelt yards away. But the crisis passes, as he wins with difficulty a sense of God's providence.

A sense of God's providence is something for which Mr Osborne clearly needs to rely on his historical imagination. This is not only because of an absence of theological belief, but because of an evident precariousness in what Dr Erikson calls 'basic trust' – the original optimism, the assumption that 'somebody is there', without which we cannot live.[19] Jimmy Porter is in quest of that assurance when, perversely, he batters away at Alison. Martin Luther finds it in his marriage with Katie: though there is a disturbing dramatic force in the Knight's repudiation of that marriage: 'Marry and stew with your nun. Most of the others have'.[20]

Still, there is no mistaking the attempt to grope after a more hopeful view of life in *Luther*. Mr Osborne appears to be denying Orwell's final pessimism when he makes *Luther* comment on the rumour that the world is going to end in 1532.

It sounds as good a date as any other. Yes – 1532. That could easily be the end of the world. You could write a book about it, and just call it that – 1532.[21]

But neither Orwell, nor Mr Osborne so far, have been able to express their intimations of hope with the force they give their eloquence of despair. Eloquence needs a response from an audience, and a despairing mood runs deep at the present time. It is all the more important to give proper attention to moments of groping after 'basic trust', the belief, as Orwell put it, that other people are more or less approachable.

To hold to that belief is often to find oneself almost overwhelmed by suffering and evil, as Gandhi was in East Bengal in 1946. 'I find', he said, 'that I have not the patience and the technique needed in these tragic circumstances.' None the less, his commitment was plain, 'I am in the midst of a raging fire and will stay here till it is put out.'[22] In Orwell's sense, Gandhi was *not* prepared to be defeated and broken up by life: and that is why he is so important for the modern world.

NOTES

1. *Look Back in Anger* (1957) pp. 93–4.
2. 'Reflections on Gandhi', in *Shooting an Elephant* (1950) p. 108.
3. *Look Back in Anger*, p. 47.
4. Ibid. p. 37.
5. 'The Art of Donald McGill', in *Critical Essays* (1951) pp. 108–10.
6. Title essay in *Such, Such were the Joys* (New York, 1953) pp. 12–17, 62.
7. 'Notes on Nationalism', in *England your England* (1954) pp. 64–5.
8. *Tribune*, 22 Mar. 1946.
9. 'Rudyard Kipling', in *Critical Essays*, p. 114.
10. Title essay in *England your England*, p. 202.
11. *Tribune*, 19 Oct. 1945.
12. 'Second Thoughts on James Burnham', in *Shooting an Elephant*, p. 162.
13. 'Reflections on Gandhi', ibid. p. 111.
14. Ibid. p. 113.
15. *Non-Violence in Peace and War*, vol. 1, ed. Mahadev Desai (Ahmedabad, 1948) p. 380.
16. *Young Man Luther*, p. 12.
17. Ibid. pp. 100–6.
18. *Luther* (1961) p. 72.
19. *Young Man Luther*, p. 114.
20. *Luther*, p. 91.
21. Ibid. p. 97.
22. *Non-Violence in Peace and War*, vol. 2, ed. Bharatan Kumarappa (Ahmedabad, 1949) p. 195.

Edwin Morgan

THAT UNCERTAIN FEELING (1958)

HAVE you felt it too? A suspicion that the present vigorously stirring situation in drama, exciting and praiseworthy though it is, must be greeted with some reservations? This feeling has grown on me, and it might be useful if I try to define these restless doubts.

The liveliness and theatrical power of the plays of John Osborne, Tennessee Williams, and Arthur Miller derive mainly from two things: vivid dialogue, and a choice of situations that are emotionally very raw and exploitable. Mr Osborne has remarked how 'we need a new language', and already this new language – racy, close to common speech, unafraid of contemporaneity, inventive in a spoken not a literary sense – is making its impact. It is brilliance and pace of dialogue that save Samuel Beckett's plays from sharing the tedium found in his novels; and the relative deadness of the dialogue in John Whiting no doubt contributes to the muffled impression his drama has so far made.

Dialogue isn't everything, but add powerful emotional situation to it and what more could anyone want? The long probing smouldering scene between Brick and Big Daddy in *Cat on a Hot Tin Roof*; Archie Rice singing the blues when he hears about Mick's death in *The Entertainer*; Eddie's agonized taunting and embrace of Rodolpho in *A View from the Bridge* – if these are not real theatre, you may ask, what is? Yet good scenes and great moments don't make a play, and for all the theatrical effectiveness of these passages, and of others that could have been instanced, there is clearly *something* wrong with the plays themselves, something that fails to satisfy, fails to convince.

Let's look at it first from John Osborne's point of view. In various pronouncements (e.g., in *Declaration,* and *International Theatre Annual No. 2*) Osborne has stressed the importance of a theatre of *feeling*. He attacks the stiff upper lip, and prefers working-class garrulousness to bourgeois reserve, just as Jimmy Porter keeps trying to sting Alison into the outward liveliness of retaliation. 'I want to make people feel, to give them lessons in feeling. They can think afterwards.' He is not afraid of being charged with sentimentality, and says that if this desire to crack open the British Way of Feeling is sentimental, he'll 'go on working towards a sentimental theatre' for the rest of his life. Now the ability to *move* an audience, a mixed audience of un-known composition, to move it and leave it shaken, is a great gift, and Osborne has this gift, to an extent that (for example) neither Eliot nor Fry has been able to show. But it's a gift that carries obligations and responsibilities. Osborne says we 'can think afterwards'. Supposing we don't make the effort – or we do make the effort and find that no very definitely formulated theme emerges – or that a theme emerges which doesn't deserve our approbation? In *Declaration* he warns us 'I shall simply fling down a few statements – you can take your pick'. This might be said by some weary verse dramatist knee-deep in symbols, but as the attitude of a prose dramatist who is professedly concerned with modern society and its ills, it shows an alarming dislike of clarity. I say 'alarming' because social and moral clarities are, above all, what we are needing, and what we are not getting. *Pathos* we get in full measure – even *Look Back in Anger* is essentially a play of pathos – but if our cheeks are all begrutten with tears and we're not sure afterwards what we've been weeping for, or we do know and feel we oughtn't to have been weeping for it, how are plays of this sort going to help change English society?

O Brecht, where art thou? But let me go further east than Brecht. In that uneven but sometimes revealing olla podrida, the 1957 Yearbook of the Big Soviet Encyclopedia, the article on British literary life contains an appreciative reference to John Osborne and other young writers for their 'sharp critique of contemporary bourgeois reality', but reproaches them in that

this critique is 'uncommitted, anarchic, and tinged with indivi-
dualistic bolshiness'. I am not concerned here with the 'uncommitted' aspect, but rather with the 'anarchic' and 'bolshy'. Jimmy
Porter's anger expends itself impotently, and we can't really
believe that anything is changed at the end of the play. Archie
Rice's final 'Why should I care?' theme-song simply hands the
tangle of thematic material the play had thrown up into the lap
of the battered audience with a wonderfully dismissive '*You* sort
that out!' *The Entertainer* succeeds as a play of feeling, but fails
as a play of ideas. The last scenes – the death of Billy, and the
whole Canadian business – are badly managed, and the play
loses its grip; it is saved at the end only by a return to pure pathos
and a Chaplinesque fade-out. Both this play and *Look Back in
Anger* are immediately stimulating, but on reflection ('they can
think afterwards') depressing, because they assume human failure
and frustration as the norm and are pervaded by strange hanker-
ings after a gauzy Edwardian past instead of some intimations of
the better society Osborne presumably (as a socialist) hopes
we'll live to see. A comparison with Chekhov (whom he has
referred to with respect) would remind us that Chekhov has this
whole dimension – his positive vision of the future of society –
which so far is absent in Osborne.

'Human failure and frustration as the norm' applies even more
strongly to Tennessee Williams. *Cat on a Hot Tin Roof* is a play
without an ending, a play that just hasn't worked itself out, a
play that seems like a giant excuse to enable the author to write
one marvellously intense scene, after which he loses interest.
Williams is concerned with a very real problem – the waste of
character which accompanies human loneliness, especially the
loneliness that grows where normal and abnormal natures are
thrown together. But once he has made it plain to us why Brick
is an alcoholic and why he has no interest in his wife, he doesn't
know what to do with any of his characters. The play is a failure
in action, or if you like in plot. Williams has himself referred to
his 'more or less static' plays (*Four Plays*, p. xii), and he often
relies a good deal on poetic atmosphere and subtly changing
mood to replace action and development of character. All right:

this is one way of doing things. But when your plays issue in such an acutely personal key as Williams' do, involving such a profound distrust of man's freedom to act, such a deliberate foregathering under a 'No Loitering' notice, you take great dramatic risks, and chiefly the risk that people must ask themselves a new question at a Williams play, not 'What will happen now to these interesting characters?' but 'What has got them all that way?' Like Osborne, Williams looks back; most of the dialogue is devoted to recollecting the past. The *really* interesting situation of *Cat*, from any central human point of view, is the situation with which the play ends, and which the author has not thought it worthwhile even to foreshadow convincingly.

The emotional hyperaesthesia which gives dramatic force to Williams and Osborne seems at times to be cherished to the point of moral anaesthesia. This can hardly be said of the earnest Mr Miller. Yet Miller's plays share the same concern with frustration, impotence, and defeat, and the same central vacuum, the lack of any bodied vision, any spur of hope whether social or metasocial, anything against which defeat and squalor and disappointment can be measured. The gloomy and ambiguous closing speech of the lawyer who acts as 'chorus' in *A View from the Bridge*, coming as it does after the passionate events of the play, is surely a most inadequate send-off. Is it even true that Eddie the longshoreman had 'allowed himself to be wholly known'? And granted that it is at least partly true, is it important? Is it *enough*, in a 'social play' of the kind he discusses in his prefatory essay?

My reservations, then, are largely moral reservations. I have reached them without examining Beckett, Genet, or Ionesco, where the problem becomes even more acute. I haven't mentioned *Cards of Identity* or *Don't Destroy Me*, where the same moral bolshiness is at work, though in different ways. My general feeling is that the vigorous plays of the 'forties and 'fifties, entertaining and striking as they are, achieve their impact at the expense of very important things – themes that have been really brooded over till they issue from the plot like light from fire, and images of something positive and inspiring (*we* never, for example, see Jimmy Porter as Alison first saw him, when 'everything about him seemed to burn, his face, the edges of his hair glistened and seemed to spring off his head. . . .').

Arthur Miller writes in his essay 'On Social Plays': 'Our society . . . is so complex, each person being so specialized an integer, that the moment any individual is dramatically characterized and set forth as a hero, our common sense reduces him to the size of a complainer, a misfit.' This is untrue. It is not 'our common sense' which does this, it is despair, or failure of nerve, or cynicism. What playwrights can do is to help to make any such despairing point of view obsolete, by reinvesting characters with more heroic qualities than at present they seem willing to dare.

John Mander

THE WRITER AND
COMMITMENT (1961)

[The author has been writing about the poetry of Thom Gunn, of which he remarks, 'Commitment is universal: the poet of subjectivity chooses to explore its inner rather than its outer face'.]

AND here, the contrast with the commitment of writers like Mr Osborne and Mr Wesker is striking. Where Mr Gunn's views are tentative and implicit, theirs are explicit and vehement. They are known to be opponents of Apartheid, the H-bomb, the British class system: and they see in Socialism the ethical standard by which these things can be judged and condemned. All this belongs, of course, to the sphere of biography rather than literary criticism. We know these things from the newspapers, from personal contact, or from hearsay: but do we know them from the plays? There are characters in Mr Osborne's and Mr Wesker's plays who express views of a similar kind. But do these views form the content of the plays concerned? And what of 'commitment'? Do those views express their authors' commitment, or ought we to disregard them and derive the commitment solely from the content of the plays? Clearly, modern methods of publicity have made such abstinence harder for the critic. It is well-nigh impossible to ignore an author's views completely and to disentangle the characters an author has created from his own biography. For many people there is no real distinction between Mr Osborne and his Jimmy Porter, Mr Kingsley Amis and his Lucky Jim, Mr John Braine and his Joe Lampton.

The Biographical Fallacy is not a new phenomenon. Mass publicity, however, is; and in consequence biography, which has always been popular as a substitute for criticism, now threatens

to replace it entirely. So far, we have not encountered this difficulty in an acute form. There is hardly anything in Mr Auden's
or Mr Angus Wilson's work that is autobiographical in the same
sense. With Orwell it is different: almost all of Orwell's best
work can be fairly termed autobiographical. His literary life-work
is best considered as extended autobiography in which the parts –
the essays as well as the *reportage* – can hardly be understood
without reference to the whole. Orwell's 'views' are omni-
present; he is always preaching, always forcing certain opinions
down the reader's throat. These opinions may be irrational and
contradictory (as I believe they are), but one cannot cite the
Biographical Fallacy against them. This is not to say that
Orwell-the-man and Orwell-the-writer are identical. No doubt
only a fraction of Orwell's actual experience underwent a trans-
mutation into art. But the art Orwell practised was autobiography;
and from the attitudes to be found there, Orwell-the-writer's
commitment can fairly be deduced. But *Look Back in Anger* and
Roots cannot be treated in this way, though both Jimmy and
Ronnie are fashioned from autobiographical material. The
commitment must be sought, not in Jimmy's or Ronnie's views,
but in the dialectic informing the plays themselves.

What, then, are *Look Back in Anger* and *Roots* about? At first
sight, they are strikingly similar; Jimmy and Ronnie are birds
of a feather. Jimmy bullies the world in general and his women in
particular for 'not caring', Ronnie does the same. Jimmy and
Ronnie campaign against apathy and complacency and deadness:
'caring' is the attitude they oppose to them. The relevant
passages are so well known as hardly to bear quotation. There is
Jimmy's, 'You see I was the only one who cared ...' from the
speech in which he describes his father's slow dying after his
return from Spain. And there is the curtain line of *Chicken Soup
with Barley*, a line that leads straight into the second play of
Mr Wesker's trilogy, when Ronnie's mother shouts at him:
'You'll die, you'll die – if you don't care, you'll die.' (I am not
suggesting that Ronnie is derivative from Jimmy as a character,
although the more ironical presentation of Ronnie may have been
dictated to some extent by the prior existence of Jimmy; each is

an original creation, and each has his function in the organism of the play concerned.) In earlier chapters, the political or social content of a work of art was something that emerged at the end of the process of analysis. But here, I think, the process can be reversed. We may start from the assumption that the 'views' held by Jimmy and Ronnie are well known, and see how these 'views' are related to the total impact of the play. And I say 'views' instead of 'content' advisedly; since analysis of the form may well show that the content, and therefore the commitment, is something very different from the views held by either Jimmy or Ronnie.

We are given a valuable hint in Mr Osborne's own comment on Jimmy at the beginning of the play: 'To be as vehement as he is is to be almost non-committal'. This suggests, before Jimmy has had time to open his mouth, that his anger may be after all, as Mother Courage puts it, 'a short one'. But we must not anticipate. There is no doubt that Jimmy's anger is vital to the economy of *Look Back in Anger*; it is Jimmy's anger that drives the play, that makes the wheels go round. It is tempting to avoid putting a moral interpretation on it at all, and to speak quite simply of Energy. The origin of this Energy is, certainly, as unclear as its direction: it is simply *there*, an elemental, devastating force. It is curious, and interesting, how the attempts to explain Jimmy's Energy fail. Jimmy has been called a frustrated artist, a repressed homosexual, a sado-masochist, a self-pitying egotist, an idealist without a cause. Yet none of these descriptions seem to help: Jimmy eludes them. But does he elude them because he is too big, or too small? Has Jimmy a hidden greatness which could turn his anger into a condemnation of the society which has no room for him? Or is Jimmy simply, as some elder critics would maintain, 'maladjusted'? Clearly, while the Energy is there and undeniable, our final judgment on the play must depend on what significance, moral and aesthetic, we attribute to it. . . .

The neurotic's is a private world, and his language a private language; the writer makes use of it at his peril. This has an evident relevance to the question of Jimmy's anger. If Mr John Osborne's *Look Back in Anger* is a study in sado-masochism (using the term strictly in the sense of 'compulsive', i.e. non-free behaviour) then the play would seem to be of considerably reduced significance. No comment of Jimmy's on the present state of society could be taken seriously. His tirades would become in fact, what to many spectators they already are: boring, irrelevant, and silly. Jimmy's appeal for 'a little ordinary human enthusiasm', and his Lawrentian outburst 'they all want to escape from the pain of being alive. And, most of all, from love . . .': these things could be written off as the attitudinising of a hysteric. The play would be reduced, in other words, to a case-history; it would hardly be worth critical consideration.

Clearly, if the play is to be taken seriously, then it must be possible to take Jimmy's 'views' seriously. It must be shown that Jimmy's 'views' are the product of his Energy battling with a society that is in some sense too small for him. He must be an eccentric, rather than an ego-centric. And modern English society's refusal of his Energy must imply a moral judgment on that society. But taking Jimmy seriously must mean, of course, taking him seriously in his dramatic context. To succeed, the play must counterpoint Jimmy against contemporary English society; and this society must be realised on the stage itself, in the persons of Alison, Cliff, Helena, and Colonel Redfern. But if the counterpointing is to work, if the play is to have an efficient dialectical structure, then the other persons of the drama must be not merely passive. Jimmy must not be allowed to erupt like a volcano, and smother Alison, Cliff, and Helena with his Energy. Weighting the scales in Jimmy's favour would unbalance the play dramatically; and it would also be untrue to the real social situation off-stage. Against present-day English society, Jimmy's chances are not good; it would be altogether too easy to let him triumph on the stage.

These would seem to be the preconditions for success: are they fulfilled? Only, I think, to a very limited extent. The passivity of the supporting characters is a weakness that has been pointed out by almost all critics of the play. Indeed, the fact that one includes Jimmy's wife among the 'supporting' characters is significant; Alison is surely as wet a character as has ever been presented on the English stage. In bullying her, Jimmy is certainly getting an easy revenge on the class he detests. Yet Jimmy is presented as a fighter, and one would expect him to relish a fight with someone of his own calibre. But does this description fit Alison's girl friend Helena? She is tougher than Alison, and very typical of her class. But Helena, as most critics have pointed out, is too much of a type: to balance Jimmy a more original character is required. More might certainly have been made of Helena's struggle with Jimmy; as it is, their relations are restricted almost wholly to the sexual plane. And Cliff, though he has his part in the economy of the play, is a disappointingly light-weight character. His significance might have been heightened, perhaps, if the serious, self-improving side of his character had been developed further. 'I'm trying to better myself,' he tells Jimmy at the beginning of the play. And later, when he decides to leave the sweet-stall, 'I think I'd like to try something else. You're highly educated, and it suits you, but I need something a bit better.' Cliff might have been made to represent the older working-class tradition of self-improvement, which Jimmy, in his refusal to accept responsibility, is betraying. As it is, Cliff is only slightly less pale a character than Colonel Redfern, who is certainly a caricature of his class, though one portrayed with a sympathy which borders on the sentimental.

The unbalance is difficult to deny; the supporting characters are simply too feeble to support Jimmy and his anger. We are back where we began: with Jimmy's all-powerful, but inchoate, and directionless Energy. The failure to realise the minor characters means that we are left with Jimmy, unqualified and undefined. But this would matter less, were the claims Mr Osborne makes for Jimmy, in the speeches he gives him, not so ambitious. The basic claim made for him is that he knows better than others 'how to live' – since it is obvious from the context that the views Jimmy expresses have his author's approval. When Helena decides to break with Jimmy, she declares 'You can't be happy when . . . you're hurting someone else', thus provoking Jimmy's 'They all want to escape from the pain of being alive . . .' But we are not encouraged to feel that Helena might be sincere in what she says, whereas we have no doubt that Jimmy is not only sincere, but making a statement of some philosophical significance. Yet, plainly, Jimmy does not know 'how to live' better than other people; it is all talk. The famous bears-and-squirrels reconciliation at the end of the play is often condemned as sentimental. But it is probably in character; it may not be 'love' in the Lawrentian meaning, as we have been led to expect, but it is the best Jimmy and Alison can do. Unfit for love, they fall back on affection. Yet this is not presented as a criticism of Jimmy, as Mr Wesker would have made it a criticism of Ronnie. Jimmy's inadequacy is never exposed to view; even in the final scene with Alison there is a tone of superiority, when it has lost all justification. Jimmy is a phoney: but we are left with the impression that his creator cannot admit the fact.

This is, perhaps, the clue to the weakness of *Look Back in Anger*. The author invested so much of his thought and experience and energy in the person of Jimmy that he had little over for the other characters. Jimmy is the reason, both for the play's tremendous initial impact, and for its ultimate failure (the same criticism can be made of *An Epitaph for George Dillon* and *The Entertainer*; they are all, at bottom, one-man plays). Some critics, and many play-goers, have denied that Jimmy is a possible character. This can only be decided by experience; and in this case the experience of the young is likely to be most instructive. There is no doubt, to my mind, that Jimmy Porters can and do exist, and that Mr Osborne's portrait is completely faithful to contemporary social reality. To this extent, his creation is a remarkable feat of the imagination.

But we are concerned with literary criticism rather than with sociology. As a play, *Look Back in Anger* is a relative success only by the standards of a shallow slice-of-life naturalism. It gives us one powerfully realised, entirely possible human being; and a setting in which the other human beings, despite the talk, are not much more than stage-furniture. And because it fails ultimately as a drama, *Look Back in Anger* fails to say anything significant about society, or about human psychology. Such values as it expresses are simply Jimmy's values, with which the author is evidently, for the purposes of the play, in agreement. The content of the play is thus reduced to Jimmy's 'views', which are too indiscriminate to be taken seriously in themselves (the 'views' in *The World of Paul Slickey* are, significantly, indiscriminate in the same way). It is, therefore, legitimate to say (without regard to questions of autobiography) that the author is committing himself in this play to Jimmy's views. In this play, if not in others, it would be just to apply to Mr Osborne what he has himself said of Jimmy Porter: 'To be as vehement as he is is to be almost non-committal'.

Mary McCarthy

A NEW WORD (1959)

AT first glance, the main actors in *Look Back in Anger* appear to be three newspapers and an ironing-board. When the curtain goes up, on a cheap one-room flat, the audience sees a pair of Sunday papers, a cloud of pipe-smoke, and some men's feet and legs protruding; more papers are scattered on the floor, and, off to one side, a woman is silently ironing a shirt. 'Why do I do this every Sunday?' exclaims Jimmy Porter, throwing his paper down. 'Even the book reviews seem to be the same as last week's. Different books – same reviews.' At the rise of the third-act curtain, months later, the two male figures are still enveloped in the Sunday papers, while a woman is silently ironing a shirt. Same scene – different girl. Nothing really changes; nothing can change. That is the horror of Sunday. Jimmy's wife, Alison, a colonel's daughter, has finally left him, but her girl-friend, Helena, has stepped into her shoes. Jimmy, a working-class intellectual, still has a hostage from the ruling class doing the washing and the cooking, and his friend, Cliff, an uneducated Welsh boy, who boards with them, is still looking on. There has been a swap of upper-class women, like the swap of posh newspapers: you put down the *Observer* and pick up the *Sunday Times* – same contents, different make-up. A blonde is replaced by a brunette, and there is a different set of make-up on the dressing-table. The two 'class' newspapers, one Liberal, one Tory, are interchangeable, and the mass newspaper, the *News of the World*, is a weekly Psychopathia Sexualis. Other fixtures in the cast of characters are some church bells outside, the unseen landlady downstairs, and a storage-tank in the middle of the flat that represents Jimmy Porter's mother-in-law – in the third act, the new girl at the ironing-board, a home-maker, has put a

slip-cover˙ on 'Mummy', which does not alter the fact that
Mummy is still present, built in to the apartment, as she is built
in to English life.

The stagnant boredom of Sundays in a provincial town, with
the pubs closed and nothing to do but read the papers, is a
travesty of the day of rest – the day which officially belongs to
the private person, who is here seen as half an inert object and
half a restless phantom staring through the bars of his prison.
Nobody can deny that this feeling of being pent-up is characteristic of Sunday, perhaps for the majority of people in Anglo-
Saxon countries. Jimmy Porter is still young enough to feel
that something *ought* to happen, something a little different, to
break the monotony. He believes that Sunday has a duty to be
interesting. John Osborne's critics, on the contrary, believe that
Jimmy has a duty not to be bored or at least not to show it, not
to keep talking about it. As Helena, who marches into the play
waving the standard of criticism, tells her friend Alison, Jimmy
will have to learn to behave like everybody else.

'Why can't you be like other people?' This extreme demand,
which always rises to the surface in quarrels between married
couples, leaps from behind the footlights to confront Jimmy
Porter; the play alerts a kind of intimate antagonism in its
audiences, as though audience and hero were a wedded pair,
headed straight for the divorce court, recriminations, lawyers,
ugly charges. Criticism has picked the play to pieces, as though
it were a trumped-up story; imagined discrepancies or improb-
abilities are pounced on ('The play is not true to life; people do
their ironing on Mondays', or 'They would have finished reading
the papers by four o'clock in the afternoon'). One critic, writing
in *The New Republic*, thinks he knows why Jimmy Porter can't
be like other people: homosexual tendencies. Nor would Jimmy
Porter, if he could reply, change a single feature of his conduct
to avoid the drawing of this inference. The play almost asks to be
misunderstood, like an infuriated, wounded person; out of
bravado, it coldly refuses to justify itself.

Jimmy Porter's boredom is a badge of freedom, and he will
not be passive about it; for him, boredom is a positive activity,

a proclamation. To be actively, angrily, militantly bored is one of the few forms of protest open to him that do not compromise his independence and honesty. At the same time it is one of the few forms of recreation he can afford; his boredom becomes an instrument on which he plays variations, as he does on his trumpet in the next room. But other people suffer, it is said. He ought not to make other people suffer because *he* is unhappy and out of sorts. No doubt, but this is unfortunately the way unhappy people are; they are driven to distribute the suffering.

For Jimmy Porter, moreover, there is a principle involved. He is determined to stay alive, which means that he must struggle against the soporific substitutes for real life that make up the Sunday programme: the steady soft thud of the iron and the regular rustle of newsprint. His friend, Cliff, keeps telling him to shut up; his badgered wife, Alison, only wants peace, a little peace, but that is what Jimmy, or a part of Jimmy, his needling, cruel voice, has decided that she shall not have. He is fighting to keep her awake, to keep himself and his friend awake, as though all three were in the grip of a deathly coma or narcosis that had been spread over all of England by the gases emanating from the press, the clergy, the political parties, the B.B.C. Jimmy Porter's gibes are a therapeutic method designed to keep a few people alive, whether they like it or not, and patterned on the violent procedures used with patients who have taken an overdose of drugs and whose muttered plea, like Alison's, is always to be left alone.

This, at any rate, is what Jimmy thinks he is doing. His voice is a calculated irritant that prevents the other characters from lapsing into torpor. For his own part, he is tired of listening to himself and would be glad to tune in on another station, where something was really happening, where there was a little enthusiasm; he would like, some time, just once, to hear 'a warm, thrilling voice cry out Hallelujah!' Instead, there is only the deadly static provided by the Sunday weeklies, the Bishop of Bromley blessing the hydrogen bomb, and the church bells ringing outside. He thinks he would like to listen to a concert of Vaughan

Williams's music, but the ironing interferes with the reception, and he irritably shuts the radio off.

'Interference' is what Jimmy detests, whether it comes from the iron, his mother-in-law, his wife's girl-friend, or the church bells. He is morbidly suspicious in any case and morbidly sensitive to 'foreign' noises. At the same time, he is unnerved by silence. The only sound he really trusts is the sound of his own voice, which he keeps turned on mechanically, almost absently, as other people keep a phonograph going. This voice is very droll and funny, which is how it placates censure; it is 'as good as a show'. But the other characters sometimes plead with Jimmy to be quiet; they cannot 'hear themselves think' or read the papers in peace or go on with the ironing because of that voice. And if it stops talking, it moves into the next room and starts blowing on a trumpet. It never runs down and when it seems to flag for a moment, it is only to gather fresh energy, like a phonograph that pauses to let the record turn over. Jimmy demands an undivided attention, even when he is absent, and he is quick to know when no one is listening. 'I'm sorry; I wasn't listening properly,' says Alison at the beginning of the play. 'You bet you weren't listening,' he retorts. 'Old Porter talks and everyone turns over and goes to sleep. And Mrs Porter gets 'em going with the first yawn.'

Behind all this is more than egotism or a childish insistence on being the centre of the stage. Jimmy Porter is a completely isolated person whose profoundest, quickest, most natural instinct is mistrust. This is the automatic, animal wariness of a creature that feels itself surrounded. Solidarity, a working-class virtue, is for him the only virtue that is real; he exacts complete allegiance and fealty from anyone who enters his life. His women appear, so to speak, wearing his colours; both girls, while they *are* his, are seen wearing one of his old shirts over their regular clothes. When Alison is found in a slip, dressing to go out, in the second act, this is proof that she is about to revert, away from him, back to her own kind. Jimmy would make his women into men if he could, *not* because he is a covert homosexual, but because, if they were men, he could trust them.

Women do not have that natural quality of solidarity that exists between men, and they have always been suspected by men for precisely this reason; women live in the artificial realm of the social and are adepts at transferring allegiances ('making new friends') and at all the arts of deception and camouflage of which the dressing-table, stage left, is the visible sign. Alison lets Jimmy down at the crucial moment of the play – a thing he finds unthinkable, as does Alison's father, Colonel Redfern. This is followed, appropriately, by another betrayal: Alison's girl-friend, Helena, seizes Jimmy for herself.

The story of *Look Back in Anger* has, from this point of view, a great deal in common with *Hamlet*. Cliff, the working-class Welsh boy, is Jimmy Porter's Horatio, who sticks to him without understanding all the fine points of Jimmy's philosophy; and the scenes Jimmy makes with Alison have the same candid brutality that Hamlet showed to Ophelia. In both cases, the frenzied mockery springs from an expectation of betrayal. Ophelia is felt to be the ally of the corrupt Court with the murderer-king at its head, of her dull brother, Laertes, and her father, that ass Polonius. In *Look Back in Anger*, brother Nigel is Laertes and Alison's mother is cast in the role of Polonius, lurking behind the arras. The fact that Alison is secretly exchanging letters with her means that she is in communication with the enemy, like that other docile daughter, Ophelia. Women cannot be trusted because they do not understand that such an act is treachery; they do it 'in all innocence'. Apart from anything else, they do not take in the meaning of a declaration of war.

Both Hamlet and Jimmy Porter have declared war on a rotten society; both have been unfitted by a higher education from accepting their normal place in the world. They think too much and criticise too freely. Jimmy, like Hamlet, might have become a species of courtier or social sycophant; that is, he might have 'got ahead'. Critics complain that he ought to have found a job at a provincial university, instead of torturing himself and his nice wife by running a sweet stall. Hamlet, too, might have settled down to a soft berth in the Court of Denmark, married Ophelia, and waited for the succession. Hamlet's tirades and asides are plainly calculated to disturb and annoy the Court. He too cannot stop talking and, like Jimmy Porter, who practises vaudeville routines, he turns to the players for relief from the 'real' world of craft, cunning, and stupidity. Both heroes are naturally histrionic, and in both cases the estrangement, marked by histrionics, is close at moments to insanity. Both have no fixed purpose beyond that of awakening the people around them from their trance of acceptance and obliging them to be conscious of the horror and baseness of the world. Both (though this is clearer in Hamlet's case) suffer from a horrible self-doubt that alternates with wild flashes of conviction, and neither wholly wills the events he himself is causing. Yet neither wants to repent whatever it is that is driving him to destroy everything in sight, and both repel pity. 'He wouldn't *let* me pity him,' said a young woman, sadly, coming out of *Look Back in Anger*. That is just the concession the play refuses to make; if the audience pitied Jimmy Porter, this would be interference.

The Entertainer is a softer play than *Look Back in Anger*. The enemy here is identified with the 'men of Suez' and the right wing generally; this, being a political grievance, is easier for the audience to sympathise with. To be angry about politics is conventional. The Suez crisis is somewhat arbitrarily linked with a family of music-hall performers whose contact with the invasion is so remote, theatrically, that the fact that they have a son 'out there', fighting, is only mentioned, like an afterthought, at the end of the third scene. On the surface, this play has far more plot than *Look Back in Anger*: Archie Rice, a down-and-out music-hall comedian, is pursued by bankruptcy and the figure of the Income Tax man; he wants to leave his old, sodden, moronic wife and marry a young girl; his daughter goes to the Trafalgar Square protest meeting against Suez and breaks her engagement; his father dies; his other son and probably his wife are going off to Canada to join some relations, while he is slated for jail. Yet much of this plot is clumsily messengered in, by telegrams, newspaper stories, straight narration, so that it seems a kind of dubious hearsay – the daughter's engagement to someone called 'Graham'; the young girl they say Archie wants to marry; even the two deaths. The relations in Canada come to life, if life it can be called in the letter that is read from them describing their TV set and their new Chevrolet Bel-Air. This is enough to tell Archie that he would rather go to jail, and it is enough for the audience to get the picture in a flash. But, with this exception, nothing that occurs on the periphery carries much conviction; the centre is Archie Rice, lit by a spot, standing before a curtain gamely doing his act, while beyond him, in the wings, there is only an empty blackness, a void of shadows. Somewhere in that void there is the Man with the Hook – death and taxes.

Jimmy Porter is 'as good as a show', and Archie, with his tipped hat and bow tie and gloves and cane and blackened eyebrows, is the grisly show itself. He is the eternal performer who enters before the variety queens and who has to hold the audience or else be jerked off the stage. His function is to keep the show going, no matter what – if a fire breaks out or the bombs start falling or somebody dies. Like Jimmy, Archie cannot stop talking; this is his professional misfortune – the commitment he has made to the management. Silence, for this old pro, is the ultimate terror; he listens intently, head cocked, for the laugh or the patter of applause rising from the darkness of the pit, to assure him that he is still there, in the spotlight, in short that he still exists. If his own voice falters, if he dries up, he is done for; the orchestra will strike up to cover the silence, and the hook will come out to claim him. All the clichés of the stage, of the old trouper who 'never missed a performance', take on in this play a quality of sheer horror.

The actor and the soldier have the same mythology; timing, co-ordination, a cool nerve, resourcefulness, are essential to the discipline. A vaudevillian like Archie Rice looks on the stage as a fort he is holding, until relief in the form of the next turn will appear. Before a performance every actor experiences a slight case of battle-nerves, and actors, like soldiers, are superstitious. In *The Entertainer* this equation between the actor and the soldier is instinctively caught and exploited for an effect of tragic pathos. The link with Suez seems strained in terms of stage-plotting, while the characters are merely talking and drinking gin, like other people. But when Archie, in costume, is revealed with a tall nude behind him, like a recruiting poster, who wears the helmet of Britannia and holds a bulldog and a trident, the grotesque relation becomes real. His fading personal fortunes are eerily identified with the fading of the Empire. His personal hollowness echoes the present hollowness of the Empire idea, and the proposed retreat to Canada signifies the shift of power. The old growling bulldog England is represented by Archie's father, an old trouper and veteran who went through the Dardanelles without a scratch and who re-enlists, as it were, when summoned by Archie to save the family's collective life; he dies at his post, performing, and his coffin is draped in the Union Jack. The old man's sacrifice, to save a 'no-good, washed-up, tatty show', is a useless expenditure. The silence that Archie fears closes in at the end; it is the death of old England. The actor is finished, and it is the audience's turn to 'have a go'.

'Don't clap too hard, we're all in a very old building' – this grim antique vaudeville wheeze which is part of Archie's stock of gags evokes another play, written at another crisis of the declining Empire, during the First World War: Shaw's *Heartbreak House*. Shaw's draughty old country house, England, which is run by a mad, drunken sea-captain, has gone down still another step with John Osborne, and become a draughty old vaudeville house at a run-down coastal resort, with an alcoholic comedian introducing a girl-show. Shaw was a man of sixty when he wrote *Heartbreak House*, and Osborne was twenty-eight, last year, when *The Entertainer* was first produced. Both men had received a bitter education in the school of poverty that made the protected assumptions of well-to-do people appear to them as a kind of ludicrous insanity. Shaw's father was a drunkard; Osborne's mother was a barmaid. Shaw got his training for the stage as a speaker at street-corners and socialist meetings; Osborne got his as an actor, often unemployed. Bravado, impatience of cant, and a gift of gab are the product of these experiences. Shaw, to the day of his death, was obsessed with waking people up, rubbing their noses in the raw facts of life, of which they seemed so incredibly ignorant; Osborne is the same, though somewhat more savage, having come from lower down in the social scale. Shaw was, of course, an inveterate entertainer; that was his calamity, like Archie Rice's. And, like Jimmy Porter, he could never give his public a rest, leave them in peace to read the paper; he was always 'at' them, telling them their faults, just as he did with his friends. The audience, toward the end, got a little tired of him, and he, no doubt, got a little tired of himself, coming on to do his turn, in his grizzled stage eyebrows and beard. More and more, as he grew older, he had the feeling that he was talking sense and no one was listening.

Throughout both John Osborne's plays there is a longing for a message, a 'new word' – for purification, simplification. Personally, like Shaw, he is a vegetarian and does not drink alcohol. Shaw thought he had a message, if he could only get people to hear it. Osborne is in a more radical fix. Shaw could not sell him simplified spelling or an easy way to socialism. There is no new word, and, if there were, nobody would listen. One of Archie Rice's sons is a conscientious objector, but he has no hope of converting anyone and does not try; being a c.o. is his way of being an odd-ball, in a family of odd-balls, and he accepts it for that, as one accepts one's face. Archie Rice's daughter has been giving art lessons to a gang of tough kids in a London Youth Club; she does not expect any good to come of it. Yet she has been moved by the Trafalgar Square meeting to the point where she feels that something *might* happen, something in fact *must* happen, some change or redemption. Hence she comes home and starts trying to redeem Archie. But Archie is way ahead of her – a nice man, friendly, but far beyond recall, off in lunar space, where no new word could reach him. The transparent gauzes and dissolving walls of the stage set explain what has happened to the home the girl has come back to and which she takes for solid. It is a transparent deception; you can see straight through it, out into the blackness. This ectoplasm of a home is inhabited by monologists; nobody listens, as the girl and the old man protest; everyone tells the same story, airs the same objections, like a collection of tired phonographs. The voices are slurred and they forget what they started to say; there was a point to be made, long ago, but it has been forgotten.

Archie, the head of this dissolving household, has been dead a long time and floated off into filmy unreal distances, beyond the pull of gravity, with the spotlight still playing on him, picking him out, like some powerful telescope. Nothing can happen to Archie any more because he is a spook, dead, as he says, behind the eyes. Archie is an eternity, steadily doing his routine, grinding out his grinning patter, like the salt-mill that fell into the sea ('You wouldn't think I was sexy to look at me, would you? No, honestly, would you, lady?'). He has heard something once (the 'warm, thrilling voice'), an old negress singing, but he was half-slewed at the time, so that his account of the message is garbled. Now he half-listens to his daughter, politely, warily, trying to get her point of view, that is, to fix the remote point in space where this new sound is coming from. Archie is not always certain when he is onstage and when he is at home; it is all a cover-up anyway. He may be dead, but he is not taken in. The last story he tells, in his final stage appearance, is a story about a little man who finds himself in eternity, in paradise, and when a saint on the welcoming committee asks him what he thinks of it, he looks around the upper regions and answers with a four-letter word. After a moment's consternation, the saint throws his arms around the little man and kisses him. He has been waiting to hear that word ever since he came there – that is, for all eternity.

What is that word, exactly? And what has John Osborne got against Heaven? The answer is very simple. The word is hell (h-e-l-l), and that is what John Osborne has to say about this other-Eden, demi-paradise, the Welfare State, where, as Archie observes ironically, 'nobody wants, and nobody goes without, all are provided for'. The anger of John Osborne, which has angered so many people, is total and uncompromising; these two plays are nothing more or less than lively descriptions of hell. Those who want to be told what is biting the playwright have only to look around them, at the general fatuity and emptiness which is so much taken for granted that it appears as normal and almost no one hopes or wishes for anything better. A good deal has been made of the fact that Osborne, in an essay published in a volume called *Declaration*, attacked the Queen and the Tories; but the Queen, as admirers of royalty are fond of pointing out, is only a symbol anyway, a symbol of the universal cover-up in which the Tories co-operate, but not the Tories alone. Osborne is no Labour-Party canvasser, offering false teeth and nationalised steel to the masses; the changes which might be effected, under present conditions, by a return of Labour to power would be minute, and Osborne knows this. To have Labour in power would make a tiny difference, a break in the monotony; a *little* reality might filter in. Osborne is a socialist who prefers working-class people to people who have never seen a flat with an outside toilet for the same reason that Shaw did: because, on the whole, they are more real; because, like Candida's father and Eliza Doolittle's father, they are shameless and unregenerate observers of what goes on around them. Sixty or seventy years ago, when Shaw began writing, such a preference appeared less shocking and mystifying than it does today, which itself is a proof that it was time someone spoke out again, plainly, and let the sound of a human voice, now evidently so unfamiliar, rattle the old building.

Charles Marowitz

THE ASCENSION OF
JOHN OSBORNE (1962)

IF one looks closely at the crotchety, constipated, hypercritical figure of Martin Luther in John Osborne's newest play, one is forcibly reminded of that fuming British malcontent, Jimmy Porter; a protestant who bitched against the Welfare State as vehemently as the theologian wrangled with the Pope. The similarities do not end there.

Despite the jump in time, the clerical context and the change of venue, the play is not (as has been charged here) a *departure* for Osborne. There is a clear link-up between Luther's sixteenth-century Germany and our time. In both, the sense of cosmic imminence is very strong. 'The Last Judgement isn't to come. It's here and now,' says Luther, and the doomsday-mountain-squatters and the nuclear-psychotics echo his words. The church-sale of indulgences is put forward as if it were a commercial advertisement, and the suggestion here is that the Catholic Church at its lowest moral ebb is an appropriate symbol for modern ad-mass culture. And who is the cleric Tetzel but a kind of bloated Arthur Godfrey pushing piety with the same unctuous-ness used to boost Lipton's Tea?

The Osborne of *Look Back in Anger* and *The Entertainer* gave us the *temperature* of social protest. And it was blisteringly hot. In *The World of Paul Slickey*, no longer content with the charged implication and the social inference, Osborne issued indictments. One of these was made out for the church. There was something compulsive in the way that Osborne humiliated his churchmen in *Slickey*. I have a stark image of an obscenely capering clergy-man shedding all the moral restraints one usually associates with the cloth. Osborne seemed to be taking it out on the church because of some fundamental failing, and it was tinged with a personal bitterness – as if Osborne himself had been let down.

The religious disturbance is implicit in all the earlier plays. In his first play, *Epitaph for George Dillon*, there is an arbitrary scene whose only purpose is to deflate the condescending, sold-on-God visitor to the Elliot home. And if we ask ourselves (as so many have) what was bugging Jimmy Porter and George Dillon, the answer would seem to be: loss of faith. Jimmy's plea for 'a little ordinary enthusiasm' and Archie Rice's reverence for that 'pure, just natural noise' emanating from 'an old fat negress getting up to sing about Jesus or something like that' both suggest a yearning for spiritual elevation. The passion that Jimmy Porter cannot muster because 'there aren't any good, brave causes left' is the very protoplasm of faith.

It is almost as if Osborne, tracing skepticism down to its roots, had to move from George Dillon to Jimmy Porter to Archie Rice to Martin Luther – almost as if they were all part of the same family. Porter was the overt cynic Dillon was fast becoming, and Archie Rice the exhausted version of both. The springs of that doubt and disillusion can be seen to issue from a sixteenth-century fountainhead. It was Martin Luther who institutionalized doubt. His Rome was the most impregnable of all Establishments – its holy orders an array of Yes Men that makes the Madison Avenue hirelings sound like rampaging individualists. Luther's won't-take-cant-for-an-answer intellect produced the revolution that Jimmy Porter could only imagine. Both threw bricks at stained-glass windows, but whereas Jimmy ran away, Luther moved in and set up shop.

Structurally, Osborne's new play is a series of taut interviews interspersed with sermons and smeared thick with cathedral atmosphere. Formalistically, Osborne (like practically every other modern playwright) appears to be under the sway of Bertolt Brecht. Like Brecht, he has strung together a series of short, stark tableaux. Like Brecht, he has backed them with evocative hangings (flags, banners, tapestries, crucifixes). Like Brecht, he employs a narrator to fill in background and make comment. Like Brecht, he has balanced the man and the social structure so that every movement of one produces a gesture from the other. But unlike Brecht, he has not endowed his play with that added intellectual dimension around which the drama may cohere. He has not, in this tart dramatization of history, furnished an underlying concept with which to interpret events.

Spectacle and rhetoric propel the play's first two acts, but by Act Three it comes to a dead stop because language which has already posited the argument, no longer has a job to perform. The only promising dramatic situation in the play concerns Luther's encouragement and subsequent betrayal of the peasants in their revolt against the lords. This is merely reported after the event in a beautifully written narrative speech which doesn't make up for the lack of action. This is the Brechtian influence at its most destructive. The dramatic climaxes are siphoned dry; characters are involved with the intellectual implications of their behavior rather than with the blood and bone of their situations. A narrative, imagistic language is giving us the 'point' of the Luther story in a series of historical passages annotated with theological footnotes. The strongest character in the second half is a Knight who helped put down the peasants' rebellion, and what gives him such presence is the fact that he has just waged war and arrives at least with the residue of an involvement. The real battle has been in Luther's conscience and we have felt only its mildest repercussions. No one has come forward to oppose our protagonist. His anti-clerical father has raged only against losing a son to the monastery. The Pope has threatened but backed down. The beaten peasants have shied off with their tails between their legs. From scene to scene we find ourselves being cheated by authenticity.

The play's final moments emphasize the dearth of development. Luther's second dialogue with Staupitz points up how little we know about either character. The friendly old churchman remains nothing more than a theological straight-man leading Luther into aphorisms and reflection. The worst-written scene in the play shows us Luther, the family man, bussing his baby and being lovingly henpecked by a thoroughly characterless wife. In place of the last-act solidification of ideas (not a desirable way to write a play, but obviously the kind of play Osborne *was* writing), we get the scene of pregnant ambiguity which invites us to moor the play in whichever dock we like, as the writer wasn't going anywhere in particular anyway.

After the tapestries and crucifixes have been struck, and the ring of the language died away, we ask ourselves what is the lesson of *Luther*. Behind peppery images like 'empty as a nun's womb' and 'the world's straining anus', we try to discern the mind of the twentieth-century playwright.

To judge by the play's final sentiments, it would seem that God is in His heaven and sometimes out of town, and if we are all patient and courageous, He may return in our lifetime. But no, surely John Osborne hasn't fashioned all this to project such a double-barreled homily. If we interpret the play's undercurrent, it is that personal faith rather than institutional dogma (commitment?) is the way to salvation. (Or if not salvation, at least to security and influence, for in his later days Luther was a much respected hellfireist who, after granting clergy permission to marry, took an ex-nun to his own cloister-bed and fathered five little Lutherans.) But all of this remains extra-theatrical speculation and no theory, no matter how valid, seems to make that necessary circuit which links the mind of the playwright to the imagination of the audience.

If the play proves nothing about Luther it proves a great deal about John Osborne. It proves that he has the ability to grasp dramatic ideas and the language to convey them on a hard, bright poetical level. Also, he can don period costumes and still hold a twentieth-century stance, and in a theatre where an historical milieu automatically produces turgid posturing, this is a real asset. His structural and intellectual shortcomings do not diminish these gifts.

Osborne, I would guess, is fishing round for a new theme – or rather a new objective correlative in which to express his old theme: personal idealism in collision with institutional dogmas. He has gravitated from anger to contemplation, and that is a healthy progress. One looks forward to his next work with exactly the same eagerness that preceded *Luther* – that preceded

Slickey – that seems to precede everything the man writes.

At the start of what promises to be the swinging sixties, Osborne remains the most ornery dramatist in England. He still smarts, seethes and occasionally rages. He refuses to conform to other people's idea of his nonconformity. He rejects the cosy club chair and the gutless protest that crackles in the lounge and smolders on the street. He still winces at the stench in his country and refuses to pretend it is only someone burning leaves in the back yard.

He is the closest thing England has to a Norman Mailer. Like the terror of Greenwich Village, he is at war with 'the shits' and will not give them any quarter. He too uses the daily newspaper as a sounding board and recently published a hate-letter to England which only a Jonathan Swift could have duplicated. When he is harassed by petty columnists, he slaps them with law suits, and has probably been involved in more litigation than William Schwenk Gilbert. He produces in me a warm sense of security, for I always feel that he is one of the few (small 'c') committed playwrights who really write out of a conviction – that it is a social and humanist conviction and not an allegiance to maintain the fashion of the irate, verbose radical – and that unlike the (capital 'C') Committed writers, he is not partial to anything except his art.

PART FOUR

Some Foreign Reviews

Harold Clurman (1957)

JOHN Osborne, an actor still in his twenties, wrote a play two or three years ago, *Look Back in Anger*, which has ... knocked ... at the door of British drama. The knock reverberated momentously through the English theatre, and its echo, slightly muted by its ocean passage, may now be heard on our Broadway shore.

I saw the play at its opening in London, where it was received by the leading critics with an excited gratitude which astonished as much as it pleased me. What the play represented to its English audience was the first resounding expression in the theatre not only of troubled youth but of the tensions within large segments of the middle class in England today. The play is contemporary in a way in which Rattigan on the one hand or Eliot and Fry on the other are not.

The play brings before us two young men of working-class origin in the English midlands who have a candy-stand concession in a local cinema. One of them – Jimmy Porter – has had a university education and acts as a self-appointed protector to his Welsh buddy, an uncomplicated person happily free of metaphysical anguish.

Jimmy is married to a pretty girl whom he feels he almost had to steal away from her family, the kind of family whose strength and graces were grounded on England's 1914 Empire. Jimmy not only resents his wife's family and all the institutions that bred them because they led to nothing but the dust and ashes of 1945; he also berates her for having lost the stamina presumed to be characteristic of her background, without having replaced it with any new values of her own – even romantically negative ones like his.

A fourth character, a young actress, represents that middle class which obstinately holds on to its customary traditions; and there is also the wan figure of Jimmy's father-in-law, bewildered and impotent in an England he no longer recognizes.

Jimmy Porter, then, is the angry one. What is he angry about? It is a little difficult at first for an American to understand. The

English understand, not because it is ever explicitly stated, but because the jitters which rack Jimmy, though out of proportion to the facts within the play, are in the very air the Englishman breathes. Jimmy, 'risen' from the working class, is now provided with an intellect which only shows him that everything that might have justified pride in the old England – its opportunity, adventure, material well-being – has disappeared without being replaced by anything but a lackluster security. He has been promoted into a moral and social vacuum. He fumes, rages, nags at a world which promised much but which has led to a dreary plain where there is no fiber or substance – only fear of scientific destruction and the minor comforts of 'American' mechanics. His wife comments to the effect that 'my father is sad because everything has changed; Jimmy is sad because nothing has'. In the meantime Jimmy seeks solace and blows defiance through the symbolic jazz of his trumpet; while his working-class pal, though he adores Jimmy and his wife, wisely leaves the emotionally messy premises.

Immanent reality plus a gift for stinging and witty rhetoric are what give the play its importance. It is not realism of the Odets or Williams kind, nor yet poetry, although it has some kinship to both. It adds up to a theatrical stylization of ideas about reality in which a perceptive journalism is made to flash on the stage by a talent for histrionic gesture and vivid elocution. While the end product possesses a certain nervous force and genuineness of feeling it is also sentimental, for it still lacks the quality of an experience digested, controlled, or wholly understood.

Someone asked me if I didn't believe the play might achieve greater dimensions if American actors were to play it in a manner now associated with the generation influenced by the Group Theatre. The question reveals a misunderstanding of the play's nature. It calls for the verbal brio and discreet indication of feeling which it receives from the uniformly excellent, attractive English cast – Kenneth Haigh, Mary Ure, Allan Bates, Vivienne Drummond.

Jimmy Porter, 'deepened' in another vein, would prove an intolerable nuisance, a self-pitying, verbose, sadistic jackanapes.

He is a sign, not a character. We accept him because in the final count he is more amusing than real. We can look beyond him and the flimsy structure of the fable in which he is involved and surmise some of the living sources in the civilization from which he issues.

That John Osborne is attached and attuned to those sources is the virtue and hope of his talent. It may take ten years for him to achieve what most people have declared he already has.

John Gassner (1960)

JOHN Osborne's *Look Back in Anger* won considerable support on Broadway for its pungent realism. The work was unmistakable evidence of new talent, and both its merits and limitations are significant. The play came to us strongly, and not altogether correctly, recommended as the first serious effort of the younger generation in England. New York critics were pleased to discover that England could still produce a work of passion and protest instead of its customary drawing-room amenities and acerbities. But some of us thought of this drama as the conclusion rather than the beginning of an era of playwriting, as a blind alley rather than as a vision of promise and advance.

The subject of the play is the despair of a generation that has only bitter memories of past betrayals of ideals. The rancorous young hero's father had fought in the Spanish civil war on the Republican side. The son, who operates a sweets stall in London, can only look back in anger and toward a void in the future. He lashes out at those who are closest to him, especially his long-suffering, upper-class wife, in a vain effort to assuage his sense of futility and stalemate. His wife leaves him at last, but with a woman's tenderness for her suffering man she returns to care for him and to try to fill the void in her own life, left by the loss of her baby.

Whatever the merits of the writing, and they are considerable, *Look Back in Anger* is limited by the nihilism of its author and the crackle and sputter of fireworks in a mist. For a play characterized by admirably sustained dialogue and taut, fragmentary conflicts *Look Back in Anger* was curiously unsatisfying. The irritation, even outrage, that I noted in the audience during the intermissions was unique in my playgoing experience. Most Broadway play-goers were fascinated by the superb performances of Mary Ure as the wife and Kenneth Haigh as the angry husband, and by the passion and expressive power of the writing. But they left the theatre desolated rather than purged.

The realism of seedy settings, vibrant acting, forthright staging, the sordid story, and the pungent dialogue was altogether appropriate here. But in the context of the play the realistic refinements are only arid achievements. There was a time, not so very long ago, when it was possible to associate realistic art with a positive attitude rather than with the negations of a *Look Back in Anger*. Positive realism is rare today, and as often as not it is indirect and ambiguous; it is a glow in the dark rather than a spacious sunburst. Only the nihilism of a Williams or Osborne releases the full voltage of realism on our stage, and the effect of the work as a whole is likely to be less gratifying than the effect of individual scenes. Direct affirmativeness produces mainly the torpid flow of such mildly optimistic liberal writings as *The Prescott Proposals*.

Equally symptomatic is the inconclusiveness present in the literature of protest. The energy of even so intense a work as *Look Back in Anger* begins to run out after the first act, and the wife's return at the end leads to no particular conclusion. John Osborne's vigorous writing cannot move ahead full steam when he presumably believes he has nowhere to go. The weakening of *Look Back in Anger* after the first act is perhaps the most con-clusive evidence we have that modern drama is in a state of crisis. Modern stage realism was the product of both anger and hope. Now only the anger provides energy; the hope, producing mostly mild problem plays and liberal tracts in dialogue, only debilitates. While Ibsen and his school led the theatre modern realism was a mark of health. Outraged Victorian moralists characterized it as decadence then and, ironically now that our professional moralists no longer trouble themselves over the state of the theatre, they may yet be proved right.

I cannot join those who consider every sign of subsiding realism a mark of progress or those who exult over this state of affairs in the contemporary theatre. We are not yet ready to dismiss realism categorically. The fact is that *Look Back in Anger* begins with the jet propulsion of stripped emotion and makes most flights of fancy and poetry in our theatre seem unexciting.

Guy Dumur (1958)

HERALDED by massive publicity launched in Chelsea and taken up by Broadway, John Osborne's play is ideally suited to the taste of the middle-class theatregoer in Britain, America and France. It is a play to reassure everyone: it attacks nothing, it demonstrates nothing. The leader of the 'angry young men' is an enfeebled disciple of Jean Anouilh. He hardly seems conscious that a very great writer of his country, D. H. Lawrence, had, more than thirty years ago, dealt with problems very similar to his own. But with what force and sincerity Lawrence did it!

Theatrical managements everywhere look above all for plays which cannot offend the vast public they want to reach. But these powerful impresarios, who know their trade well, know equally well that to keep their audiences' conscience clear, plays have to be decked out with little problems suited to the taste of the day. In *La Paix du Dimanche* – the English title, *Look Back in Anger*, is more pretentious – it is the problem of marriage between young people of different classes. A worker's son, embittered and magnetic; a colonel's daughter, pure and conventional. *Petit bourgeois* against *petit bourgeois*. The gentle colonel's daughter leaves her explosive husband for a while, gives birth to a child which must needs be born dead, and comes back home to the flat just a few moments after it has been vacated by her best friend, an actress. Compared with such dramatic technique that of Bernstein seems daring, that of Anouilh positively *avant-garde* ...

Nothing is said. ... In the careful production by Raymond Gérome, who seems eager to take over from Raymond Rouleau on the boulevards, there is a lot of shouting and business to fill the gaps. Pierre Vaneck, who could be a good actor if he were just once in his life well directed, rants his way through the play without ever managing to place his character for us. But how could he? I willingly agree that a certain number of specifically British touches give the character and the play some consistency – in the original language. But the boredom of the English Sunday, the colonel back from India and so on – can they be translated into French? Nothing is left but a little superficial exoticism which makes the public feel they are getting the real thing.

In any case, after the films of James Dean and the novels of Françoise Sagan, we are now at the third stage of journalistic speculation on youth. The film, the novel and now the theatre have taken some real anxieties of youth, some questions which confront youth, and have returned only a pale, undisturbing image of them. By thus sacrificing truth in order to preserve the clear consciences of the middle-class public, this anodyne image allows them to go home reassured. The screen darkened, the book closed, the curtain fallen, everything returns to the *status quo*. It is not with James Dean or John Osborne – or their like – that the sins of an unjust world will be absolved.

PART FIVE

Points of View

Allardyce Nicoll (1962)

'THE first night of John Osborne's *Look Back in Anger* at the Royal Court on May 8th, 1956, was a turning-point in the history of the modern British theatre.'

This statement, frequently repeated in diverse forms during recent years, has now become a truism: 'turning-point', 'break-through', 'upsurge', 'revolution' are all terms which seek to define the quality of the new movement. Concerning the positive value of its achievements there has been variety of opinion. Some critics have been inclined generally to condemn, although only a very few in the hostile camp fail to applaud certain particular plays inspired by the revolutionary objectives. Other critics are excitedly enthusiastic in general, although even the most zealous have been forced to express their doubts; Kenneth Tynan wonders whether the break-through has not broken down, and Peter Brook admits that

even Noël Coward in making his attack on what we know to be an inadequate *new* theatre is really saying – despite himself – not that the old theatre was good – but that the new one is almost as bad – and in its own way, just as middle-class.[1]

Wherein lies the truth we, as contemporaries, cannot tell with assurance; only time's perspective can give us that answer; and accordingly little real profit can accrue from trying to estimate which of these plays will remain memorable and which will slip into oblivion. One thing, however, contemporaries may do is to set the plays of their age against the theatre's historical background, and perhaps there may be some virtue in an attempt briefly to view the products of this modern dramatic movement, not in isolation, but in association with the playhouse of the past.

For this there is ample justification. All the terms, from 'turning-point' to 'revolution', applied to these plays of the past five or six years stress their newness, emphasise that the younger playwrights have boldly made a complete cleavage between their efforts and the dramatic styles current in the years preceding

1956. We are, then, invited to make the comparison. But this comparison, if it is to be something more than a vague pitting of 'old' against 'new', demands that we should look, as objectively as possible, at the relationship between the 'new' endeavours and at the whole progress of the stage during our century.

Just as soon as we take this approach, casting our gaze backwards, we suddenly discover, to our surprise, that many of our younger playwrights have, in fact, leap-frogged back over the early fifties and the forties and landed in the Edwardian and Georgian eras. Outwardly, of course, they appear to inhabit a distinct world of their own, yet the number of earlier themes which they have chosen to re-exploit seems to demonstrate that in the period 1900–30 they have found metal which to them is attractive.

An immediate example presents itself. Basically, *Look Back in Anger* deals with the theme of a gently nurtured girl who is strangely magnetised by a lower-class intellectual; her mother, we are told, has been and remains vigorously opposed to the marriage, but the girl's retired-officer father, although puzzled, exhibits remarkable understanding; by the side of the ill-assorted pair stands, or lounges, an ineffective, faithful, devoted friend. Now, all the elements, or ingredients of this theme are exactly similar to those which were largely cultivated between 1900 and 1930. Again and again, as in *The Best People* (1926) by David Grey and Avery Hopwood, we find a gently nurtured Marion intent on marrying an 'intellectual' chauffeur Henry, while her father, a retired military man, stems the tide of rigid feminine opposition with perplexed understanding. *The Best People* does not exhibit a sentimentally devoted friend, but many other plays include him in the picture. Generally, the plots were worked round to a happy ending, but in some at least the atmosphere remained dark. The heroine of John Galsworthy's *The Fugitive* (1913), for instance, is a young wife, Clare Dedmond, who elects to run off with a writer Kenneth Malaise, described, in terms not unreminiscent of Jimmy Porter, as 'a tall man, about thirty-five, with a strongly-marked, dark, irregular, ironic face, and eyes which seemed to have needles in their pupils' – whose vitupera-

tive comments on the world are often akin to those we listen to
in *Look Back in Anger*:

Blessed be the respectable! May they dream of – me! And blessed
be all men of the world! May they perish of a surfeit of – good
form! . . . Not a word, not a whisper of liberty from all those
excellent frock-coated gentlemen – not a sign, not a grimace.
Only the monumental silence of their profound deference before
triumphant Tyranny.

Clare and Malaise sink down in their attic, and eventually she
commits suicide.

Obviously, Osborne's play shows a vigorous drive which
distinguishes it from most other preceding works of a like kind;
obviously, too, it strikes a new note in concentrating upon Jimmy
Porter's uninhibited egoism. Whereas almost all the earlier plays
had treated the theme as a story, starting at the beginning and
moving to a determined close, *Look Back in Anger* omits the
preliminaries, focuses attention upon the life being led by the
pair, and ends inconclusively, with the abject degradation of the
girl at Jimmy Porter's feet. Nevertheless, despite the vast
difference in atmosphere, the fact that this play deals with a theme
freely exploited during the first decades of the century and only
occasionally handled by dramatists of the forties and early fifties
deserves to be noted, particularly since *Look Back in Anger* does
not in this respect stand alone.

NOTES

1. 'Search for a Hunger', *Encore*, VIII (1961) 12.

Laurence Kitchin (1960)

THE fact remains that it was the Royal Court which made the
breakthrough with John Osborne's *Look Back in Anger*. It was

submitted through their normal channels in 1956, read by George Devine, their Artistic Director, whose experience of European drama in association with Saint-Denis scarcely revealed a destiny as patron of Porterism, and accepted for production. The content of the play is such that it would have stood not the slightest chance of acceptance by any front-line theatre in Central London in 1956. In effect it would have been censored, not by the Lord Chamberlain but by the managements, on the grounds that it departed too far from their estimate of public taste to warrant the gamble of production. How wrong they would have been was quickly shown by the success of an excerpt on television, which boosted receipts at the Royal Court in time to rescue the entire English Stage Company venture.

Aside from Devine's act of selection, the breakthrough had been achieved strictly from below. It is most unlikely that the founders, Lord Harewood and Ronald Duncan, with a hopeful eye on literary establishment figures like Angus Wilson and Nigel Dennis, can have anticipated a shot in the arm for drama by way of a Redbrick failure who calls his brother-in-law 'the straight-backed, chinless wonder from Sandhurst' and derides the sacrosanct intellectual weekly papers. The historic Court Theatre seasons of 1904–7, in so far as they involved Murray, Masefield and Galsworthy as well as Shaw and impinged on the building's recent tradition of Pinero farces, were high-toned affairs. Half a century later, Eliot, who had once hit on a great contemporary theme* in *Murder in the Cathedral,* seemed resigned to addressing the more genteel West End audiences in verse they could no longer distinguish from prose. But something was banking up under the stodgy surface of life in mid-century England. While elections came increasingly to depend on the floating vote of white-collar workers uncertain what social class they belonged to, politics were conducted by Conservative and Labour spokesmen, sometimes from the same public schools, in the manner of arguing lecturers at the London School of Economics. It was not the State but the working class, having benefited from wartime mobility and post-war welfare legislation, which was withering

* Cf. Cardinal Mindszenty.

away. Hunger, the prime mover of all radical politics, was no longer a major issue. It was soon to be replaced by galloping consumption and the era of organized greed. People were growing up to whom *Waiting for Lefty* was a period piece, war heroes a bore, the Royal Family an institution exploited with tawdry philistinism in the less literate magazines, the British Empire a dangerous fiction which got their brothers killed in Cyprus. State education was giving more and more of such people the intellectual equipment to criticize the society they had to cope with, and they were beginning to use it. Unless they intended to devote their lives to some form of artistic activity in England, hunger was something other people, in undeveloped countries, suffered from. Much more of a threat, to well-fed young people taking material welfare for granted, would be the known danger of nuclear destruction. Self-preservation would incline them to put that political issue above all others, certainly above the stresses of a shrinking empire.

People tend to rationalize their dislike of things which get in their way. 'Hell', in Sartre's words, 'is other people.' As parents get in the way of the young in any society, we shall not be surprised to find them targets of the new English drama, as they had been of the American. The Establishment, however, is a specifically English concept, the existence of which has to be taken account of if we are to distinguish these playwrights from their transatlantic masters and colleagues. If something of the kind, an élite with formidable powers of adaptation – enough to recruit two poets of pre-war Leftist sympathies to post-war professorships at Oxford – really does exist, it would function in a manner to be understood only by insiders or by people on close terms with aristocratic tradition. If it doesn't, it would be a convenient scapegoat for the frustrations of any impatient arriviste. Hence, perhaps, the contempt which mixes with any sympathy we feel for the hero of *Look Back in Anger*. The sympathy is aroused by Jimmy Porter's generous impulse towards a loyalty beyond the bourgeois family ideal. He shares his home with a friend and grieves at an old woman's death. His ill-treatment of his wife can partly be condoned as the by-product of a collision of values;

she, after all, has been cradled in privilege and should, in theory, have the wider human sympathy. But his job selling sweets in a market seems a self-imposed misuse of education, a gesture of self-pitying exhibitionism. He is less angry than petulant, a reincarnation of Mackenzie's Man of Feeling in a Bratby setting. If the Establishment exists, we are not satisfied that it is sacrificing anything indispensable by excluding Porter; if not, then he is a failed arriviste with a chip on his shoulder. Three years later we are to feel much the same about Walter Lee in *A Raisin in the Sun*, a Negro chauffeur whose only criticism of the dollar philosophy arises from the fact that he resents his employer getting a bigger cut. Both Osborne and Lorraine Hansberry are putting a valuation on their characters above what is made good in the theatre.

Although *Look Back in Anger* may date as quickly as Coward's *The Vortex*, just as *The Entertainer* is a kind of *Cavalcade* in reverse, it tapped sources of resentment which could be turned to creative theatrical use. A young Australian painter brought up in a remote mining community tells me that Porter's sardonic quotations from the Sunday papers at the start of the play gripped his attention instantly, because they expressed feelings which he had long been disturbed by himself. This artist, who has worked in an advertising agency, scorns civilized leisure in England as 'pottering about in a rose garden under a leaden sky', admires the neo-romantic novels of Lawrence Durrell, enjoys the most lavish Stratford-on-Avon embellishments of Shakespeare and considers Mary Ure the ideal contemporary beauty, is of working-class origin and represents the livelier elements in a mid-century audience. What he found in Osborne was a kind of safety-valve, a spokesman of protest. But I think we can already claim two dramatic, as opposed to sociological virtues in Osborne: his diction, and his compassionate rendering of characters he believes to be misguided. In repertory theatres all over the country Porter's tirades, longer than anything recently tolerated in English plays for the commercial market, were listened to with rapt attention even by people who strongly disapproved of him. The Colonel, his father-in-law, who might so easily have been a stereotype on the lines of Low's Colonel Blimp, is treated sympathetically enough to give older people a foothold in the disorder.

James Gindin (1963)

THE assumption that one cannot fully appreciate the plays of Osborne, Wesker, and other contemporary British dramatists unless he has been part of or has intimately known the specific society they present has frequently appeared in reviews, criticisms, and comments about the plays. Although the work of Osborne and Wesker has been praised as an energetic antidote to a theater long dominated by ingenious productions of the classics or insipid little comedies assuming that manners have really not changed since 1914, the praise has centered on the notion that these new plays are sociological statements, presentations of how a heretofore neglected part of British society lives and thinks. Both Osborne and Wesker do set their plays in contemporary societies unfamiliar to Mayfair, but the plays are essentially emotional and dramatic statements that apply far beyond the realm of a particular time and place. Osborne's first play to be produced, *Look Back in Anger* (1956) . . . is less a play about the rebellion of the educated young man of the lower classes against current society than a play about what it means to give and receive love. Jimmy Porter does rant against bishops and 'posh' Sunday papers, against any form of aristocratic gentility or pretense, but his invective is part of a plea for human honesty and vitality, for people to live emotionally as fully and as deeply as they can. He may berate his wife for the genteel background she cannot help; but he is really hurt by her emotional nullity when she ignores the illness of the old woman who established them in the sweet stall. When Helena, Jimmy's mistress, leaves him because his wife Alison has returned, Jimmy, in his frustration, voices what is both the play's major theme and its principal indictment of society:

They all want to escape from the pain of being alive. And, most of all, from love. I always knew something like this would turn up – some problem, like an ill wife – and it would be too much for those delicate, hot-house feelings of yours. It's no good trying to fool yourself about love. You can't fall into it like a soft job, without dirtying up your hands. It takes muscle and guts. And if you can't bear the thought of messing up your nice, clean soul, you'd better give up the whole idea of life, and become a saint. Because you'll never make it as a human being. It's either this world or the next.

Both Helena and Alison understand what Jimmy is saying, and they are able to love him, not because they agree with his attacks on religion or other forms of hardened and genteel abstractions in society, but because they recognize and ultimately respond to his human energy. The game of squirrels and bears which Jimmy and Alison play seems, at first, a trivial evasion of the complexities found in any marriage. But at the end of the play the game becomes a statement of the nature of human love – the willingness to immerse oneself completely in creatureness, to share the pain and the pleasure of the limited animal. . . .

Jimmy Porter's famous statement about causes, in *Look Back in Anger*, is as personally revealing as it is politically pointed:

I suppose people of our generation aren't able to die for good causes any longer. We had all that done for us, in the thirties and the forties, when we were still kids. There aren't any good, brave causes left. If the big bang does come, and we all get killed off, it won't be in aid of the old-fashioned, grand design. It'll just be for the Brave New-nothing-very-much-thank-you. About as pointless and inglorious as stepping in front of a bus. No, there's nothing left for it, me boy, but to let yourself be butchered by the women.

The statement expresses both political skepticism and personal frustration. It is both a comment on society and a way for Jimmy to express the anger churning within him, an anger that originates in his inability to communicate with others as fully and meaningfully as he feels. And, in addition, the last sentence of the passage defines the only realm, as the whole play illustrates, in which communication can be meaningful or important. In part, a vast and complex world has made specific and limited communication the only kind possible for man. But, in part also, Jimmy Porter is the kind of person who needs the specific anchor and the intensity that only a relationship with an individual can provide. Causes are, and always were, too abstract for people like Jimmy. And one need not know the Midlands or the history of the International Brigade in Spain to recognize that.

An Osborne Symposium (1966)

JOHN OSBORNE'S *Look Back in Anger* opened at the Royal Court Theatre on May 8, 1956. Ten years later, we [at the Royal Court] asked a number of prominent writers and directors how they would sum up his contribution to the British theatre. Here are some of their answers:

'John Osborne didn't contribute to the British theatre: he set off a land-mine called *Look Back in Anger* and blew most of it up. The bits have settled back into place, of course, but it can never be the same again.' (Alan Sillitoe)

'Long before Oedipus there were Oedipus complexes, long before Hamlet there were gloomy Danes. But the day the figure took shape in a poet's mind, the day he got a name, the world acquired a new reference. It need not have happened. The right imagination isn't always there. John Osborne's achievement is that one day he gave form where no one else saw that form lay. But I hate the word achievement. John Osborne is also impatient, restless, courageous and colossally talented. It is his potential today that matters even more.' (Peter Brook)

'John Osborne's passion saved the English theatre from death through gentility. At a time of uncertain and hovering formal experiment, he has shown that the conventional theatre can still extend its emotional and verbal range beyond what we had any of us hoped. But above all, in an age when the conventional pay lip-service to humanism, he has challenged humanistic hypocrisies by demanding and obtaining a complex compassion for a wide range of the least lovable, least cosy and least glamorous of human beings.' (Angus Wilson)

'A theatre that wishes to stay alive needs passion and con- temporary relevance (sometimes known, sneeringly, as "ephe- meral journalism"). Elegance, good taste and verbal mellifluence, though excellent qualities in themselves, are inadequate sub- stitutes. John Osborne supplied the missing ingredients at a time when it seemed that their absence was no longer even noticed. (John Arden)

' "We owe so much to you," Staupitz tells Luther in the last act of John's play. We all do. John Osborne brought back honour, substance and dignity to a theatre which had been fed for decades on "shells for shells, empty things for empty men". John was the first, the breakthrough of the dramatists who have crowded in since 1956. But their breakthrough could only have happened by the authority and humanity of his voice. He is unique and alone in his ability to put on the stage the quick of himself, his pain, his squalor, his nobility – terrifyingly alone.' (Tony Richardson)

'The strength of his start was a deliberate parochialism. Instead of exploiting the deep, narrow ground he had defined – as his many imitators persist in doing – Osborne moved into history, into societies and styles of feeling radically different. Witness his return to Lope de Vega, the dramatist of a complex, hierarchic society – it, too, poised on the edge of decline.' (George Steiner)

Lindsay Anderson (1956)

IT is over ten years now since we (the junior officers) nailed a red flag to the roof of the mess at the foot of Annan Parbat, to celebrate the glorious news from home (I mean of course the result of the 1945 election). The colonel did not approve, but even he seemed to feel that a new era might be upon us; and no disciplinary action was taken.

It is also over ten years since Humphrey Jennings, in a film made for the British government, linked the lives of a farmer and an engine driver, an R.A.F. pilot, a coal miner, and a baby called Timothy. It is as beautiful a film today as it was then, but it has gained sadness; for the questions it asked about the future do not seem to be getting the hoped-for answers. From one point of view this is paradoxical. We have had our social revolution: we have a fine system of social security: and our technological achievements are something to be proud of. How then to explain the prevalence of cynicism, the baffled idealism and the emotional fatigue? Why are so many young voices resentful and defeatist rather than pugnacious and affirming?

I suppose people of our generation aren't able to die for good causes any longer. We had all that done for us, in the 'thirties and 'forties, when we were still kids. There aren't any good, brave causes left. If the big bang does come, and we all get killed off, it won't be in aid of the old-fashioned, grand design. It'll just be for the Brave New-nothing-very-much-thank you. About as pointless and inglorious as stepping in front of a bus . . .

Most critics have attempted to write off John Osborne's hero (this is a quotation from *Look Back in Anger*) as a negligible, bad-mannered young bounder, 'racked with uncertainty and rotten with self-pity'. Predictably, they have shirked the task of analysing his bounderishness: the writer in the *Times Literary Supplement*, from whom I have taken this comment, can find no virtue either in Jimmy Porter or the play, even though he admits that 'there is something about this nagging young man which audiences recognise as giving him some vital connection with the social system'. As to what this 'something' is, we are not enlightened; characteristically this is the end, not the beginning, of the examination of the play.

In so far as Jimmy Porter's grievances are social at all (and it should be realised that the play is primarily the study of a temperament), they are not material grievances. The young people who respond so unmistakably to *Look Back in Anger* are responding to its outspoken attacks on certain venerable sacred cows, and also to its bitter impatience with the moral vacuum in which, they feel, public life, and cultural life, is today being conducted. The class resentment is only part of it. If there 'aren't any good, brave causes left' (or if that is the feeling in the air), the fault is not so much that of the Right, the Tory element in politics and art, as of the Left, the progressives, the liberals in the broadest sense of that long-suffering word. The manner in which the British political Left has muffed its chance to capture the imagination and allegiance of the nation is too obvious to need dwelling on: from the peaceful revolution of '45 to 'You Can Trust Mr Attlee', and Mr Gaitskell in pin-strip trousers helping with the family washing-up, the descent has been sure, steady and well-publicised. Less easily – or at least less often – remarked has been the steady draining away of vitality from what we may call the cultural left, its increasing modishness, and its more and more marked aversion from emotional simplicity or moral commitment.

'We are all existentialists nowadays, at least in the same vague, popular sense that it was ever true to say we were all socialists . . .' This is the prevailing tone – over-allusive, fatigued, intellectually snobbish – of the *New Statesman* intellectual of today; while the indefatigable Mr Kingsley Martin, on the front page, continues to chastise the Labour Party for its lack of realism, and to warn it that it may 'drift further and further away from the realities of working-class life'.[1] We cannot but smile at such wild discrepancies, but really this sort of thing is sad rather than funny; and particularly because, of the two remarks, it is the second that is outdated. (The contemporary liberal intellectual is far less diverted by the realities of working-class life than by the variations between 'U' and 'Non-U' usage.)

A particularly pregnant example of the kind of debilitation I am describing is offered by the recent (August 18, 1956) review in the *New Statesman* of the 'Family of Man' exhibition. 'What strikes one most', writes Mr John Raymond, 'about this amazing cross-section of men and women, is its unity – a unity of fear.' Affirmation and the pursuit of happiness (which are the theme of the exhibition) being out of fashion, Mr Raymond stands to make a distinctly smarter impression if he jettisons Mr Steichen's statement, and substitutes something more up-to-the-minute of his own. The crucial passage in this argument so perfectly crystallises its pseudo-liberal attitude that readers must bear with me while I quote it in full.

What is Mr. Steichen's message? 'All men are created equal'; 'No man is an island entire of himself'; 'Where there is neither Greek nor Jew, circumcision nor uncircumcision'; 'We must love one another or die'? Judging by the Bomb that ends the whole affair, Auden's discarded line appears to be the text that the sponsors are bent on hammering home. If only Timbuctoo can learn to love Old Trafford, the lion will lie down with the lamb, our bombs can be beaten into atomic ploughshares and Walt Whitman's 'new city of friends' can be turned into a reality. Such a jejune *motif* does poor justice to the riches of this collection, even when eked out by the trite international maxims that stud the walls – 'The world of man dances in laughter and tears' (Kabir); 'Clasp the hands and know the thoughts of men in other lands' (Masefield); 'Eat bread and salt and speak the truth' (Russia) . . .

Such accomplished perversity demands analysis if its subtleties are to be fully appreciated. Confronted by the tremendous issues raised by this exhibition, the enlightened Mr Raymond is at no loss for a protective shield of sophisticated cross-references. His piece is headed 'All The Conspirators' – a quotation from *Julius Caesar* which is wholly inapposite, but has the merit of connoting

Shakespeare and (more important) the first novel of Christopher Isherwood. The reference to Auden settles us even more firmly within the charmed circle: this gospel is limited not just to the (comparatively large) number of people who can pick out Auden's line from the group of quotations listed at the beginning of the paragraph, but to the selecter élite who are aware that Auden has omitted the line from the latest edition of his short poems. His position of cultural superiority thus established – Walt Whitman is another O.K. reference, and may safely be patronised – Mr Raymond can proceed confidently to dismiss as a 'jejune *motif*' such poetic conceptions as the lion lying down with the lamb; the sword beaten into the ploughshare; and Whitman's 'New city of friends'. This is the point where the hard work of writing a criticism of the exhibition is smoothly side-stepped; instead of pointing out where Mr Steichen fails to measure up *poetically* to the texts he has chosen, Raymond dismisses the texts themselves, and with them an aspiration which has long found a place in the hearts of men, and still does today. The slickness with which this dismissal is effected is alarming, because it shows Raymond's sense that he is writing with, not against the current. It needs only the word bomb with a capital 'B', and the facetious jingle of Timbuctoo and Old Trafford to discredit the positive ideal of human brotherhood which is the essential inspiration of the whole exhibition.

I have given care to an examination of this passage, not because in itself Mr Raymond's reaction to 'The Family of Man' is very important, but because of his ability skilfully to express the social and cultural attitudes of his class and time. The really shocking thing about such a piece is that nobody is shocked by it. (The only comment it aroused among readers of the *New Statesman* was a letter pointing out that a quotation from Schiller had been wrongly attributed to Goethe.) The commitments, in fact, of the liberal intellectuals are now so taken for granted that they have ceased to have any force whatever; and to speak out for them is to run the risk of appearing simple. Mr Raymond can end his review with a pessimistic quotation from Lord Russell – 'Brief and powerless is Man's life . . .' – without fear of arousing the slightest protest from the readers of a radical left-wing periodical. His style, though intellectually more pretentious, echoes the uncommitted Mr Cooke twenty years before him: sceptical, amused, implicitly mistrustful of affirmation, even while continuing to pay indulgent lip-service to it.

NOTES

1. Both these quotations are taken from the same issue of the *New Statesman*, Dec. 1955.

Ronald Duncan (1960)

IT is true to say that we have produced a great number of plays which would not otherwise have been presented, but I do not think our playwrights have done anything new. I remember writing to John Osborne to congratulate him on *Look Back in Anger* two or three months before it was produced. It was articulate, aggressive, and a splendid statement of the sort of frustration a social anarchist feels in a Welfare State. It may well be that the immediate post-war era will come to be symbolized by Jimmy Porter. But when Mr Tony Richardson tells me that in his opinion 'Osborne is the best dramatist since the Restoration' I can only regret Mr Richardson, and feel sorry for Mr Osborne. It is not kind to give a man who has genuine talent the reputation of genius, when he does not possess it. Osborne will take his place beside Rattigan and beneath Coward. That is no disparagement. It is simply silly for anybody, including ourselves who promoted *Look Back in Anger*, or the various plays that have imitated it, to claim that it broke any ground that had not been ploughed by Ibsen, harrowed by Shaw, and trodden pretty bare by the little theatre of the 1930s. It is nearly sixty years since Max Beerbohm drew a cartoon of Bernard Shaw taking his clothes to a pawn shop . . . 'Come I've handled these goods before,' says the pawnbroker. 'Coat Mr Schopenhauer's, waist-coat Mr Ibsen's: Mr Nietzsche's trousers . . .' To which Shaw can only reply 'But look at the patches'. There is nothing new in social realism. It is true that proletarian drama is now more fashionable, but a change in fashion should not be confused with a revolution in taste. Stravinsky, Pound and Picasso did cause a revolution in taste. They made something new. We have not achieved that.

The so-called 'kitchen-sink' dramatists are still writing within the convention of *Mrs Tanqueray*. They have swopped the drama of duchesses and cucumber sandwiches for bus drivers and empty sauce bottles. But to invert a convention is not to break it. It is fair to say that they have made the working class articulate, but have they found what it is the working class has to say? Person-ally I have a shrewd suspicion that the working class is composed of human beings, and not a mere collection of puppets with a petty social grievance. I don't know of any play that achieves this expression. Perhaps it will never be written now, since the working class is fast losing its identity in the morass of the middle class, and has few other aspirations.

Tom Milne (1960)

A PLAY like *Look Back in Anger* creates a world which, in essence, is familiar to us (reality, rather than an imaginative *dislocation* of reality), and it becomes easier for the mind to sidetrack on to an element which may be more pleasing to it than the main theme of the play. Constant reference is made, even by people who liked the play, to Jimmy Porter's *self-pity*, his *neurotic* behaviour, his *cruelty* to his wife. This makes non-sense of the play; Jimmy Porter is devoid of any neurosis or self-pity, and the play is summoned up in his cry against a negative world, 'Oh heavens, how I long for a little ordinary human enthusiasm. Just enthusiasm – that's all. I want to hear a warm, thrilling voice cry out Hallelujah! Hallelujah! I'm alive.' (How Jimmy would have responded to Beatie Bryant in the closing moments of *Roots* . . .) Would *Look Back in Anger* have been the success it was if people had been forced to listen to this damning indictment of themselves as dead souls, instead of being allowed to stray into less dangerous channels (guying of English Sundays, excitingly turbulent sex-life, downtrodden and maltreated wife, etc.)?

Stuart Hall (1959)

Look Back in Anger was painful in its accuracy and immediacy, even for those people who would *not* ever have agreed that 'there were no brave causes left'. Osborne struck a representative note, he summed up the sense of inverted rage, the bitter raging against the cramped, *pusillanimous* forms of life which stifled Jimmy Porter. If Porter was unbearable, as the stiffer critics said, it was because many of us were on the edge of finding all our relationships unbearable. And what we found in *Look Back in Anger* was the language which, at least at that moment, contained something of our sense of life. Constantly critical, it yet called out something more than a reaction in us: it gave us lessons in feeling.

Arthur Miller (1957)

Look Back in Anger to me is the only modern, English play that I have seen. Modern in the sense that the basic attention in the play was toward the passionate idea of the man involved and of the playwright involved, and not toward the surface glitter and amusement that the situation might throw off. That play – and I'm not judging it now in terms of aesthetic fact – seems to me to be an intellectual play . . . and yet it seems to have no reflection elsewhere in the theatre.

QUESTIONS

1. What are the young men angry about?

2. Give your own account of Jimmy Porter's anger.

3. Outline the political and social situation of Britain in the mid 1950s. Was a wave of protest in the arts a predictable reaction to it?

4. It has been said that *Look Back in Anger* is due for revival 'in modern dress'. How far does the play now seem to you a period piece?

5. How far do the attitudes of Jimmy Porter seem to reflect those of John Osborne?

6. In *Look Back in Anger* protest is inextricably mixed with nostalgia. What is Osborne nostalgic for, and how far does this square with the protest?

7. 'A formal, rather old-fashioned play.' Do you think John Osborne's later judgement of *Look Back in Anger* justified?

8. *Look Back in Anger* has been described as a monologue play, with only one fully realized character. Is this a fair account?

9. To what extent was the 'new drama' initiated in Britain by *Look Back in Anger* really revolutionary compared with what had gone before?

10. Outline the role of the English Stage Company in the development of the 'new drama'.

11. Explain the idea of 'committed' art. Is this an adequate formula for Osborne's work?

12. Compare Osborne's anger and its objects with those of George Orwell.

13. What points of contact are there between Osborne's drama and the contemporary American plays of Arthur Miller and Tennessee Williams?

14. Do the reviews of such American critics as Mary McCarthy, Harold Clurman and John Gassner offer any fresh insights into *Look Back in Anger* which have escaped British writers?

SELECT BIBLIOGRAPHY

WORKS OF JOHN OSBORNE

Look Back in Anger (Faber & Faber, 1957; Criterion Books, 1957).

Epitaph for George Dillon, by John Osborne and Anthony Creighton (Faber & Faber, 1958; Criterion Books, 1958).

The Entertainer (Faber & Faber, 1957; Criterion Books, 1958).

The World of Paul Slickey (Faber & Faber, 1959).

A Subject of Scandal and Concern (Faber & Faber, 1961).

Luther (Faber & Faber, 1961; Criterion Books, 1961).

Plays for England (Faber & Faber, 1963).

Tom Jones: a Screenplay (Faber & Faber, 1964; revised ed., Grove Press, 1964).

Inadmissible Evidence (Faber & Faber, 1965).

A Patriot for Me (Faber & Faber, 1966).

A Bond Honoured (Faber & Faber, 1966).

STUDIES OF THE MODERN LITERARY SCENE

Contemporary Theatre, Stratford-upon-Avon Studies 4 (Edward Arnold, 1962).

A collection of nine essays, mainly by academics interested in the drama, and devised at the Shakespeare Institute, Stratford-upon-Avon. The subjects are all from the twentieth-century British drama, mainly post-1956, but including also Shaw, T. S. Eliot and modern poetic drama, as well as some sidelong glances at Anouilh, Brecht, Pirandello, contemporary Irish drama and the role of television in drama today.

Declaration, ed. Tom Maschler (MacGibbon & Kee, 1957).

Eight long essays by leading figures among the 'angry young men' at the time when the term and the idea of 'anger' were most in vogue. The contributors include John Osborne, the critic Kenneth Tynan, the director Lindsay Anderson, the novelists Doris Lessing and John Wain, and the philosophical journalist Colin Wilson. Their contributions, taken together, give a fair idea of what 'protest' in the mid 1950s thought it was about, and of how much (or how little) the leading spokesmen of committed left-wing art had in common.

The Encore Reader, ed. Charles Marowitz, Tom Milne and Owen Hale (Methuen, 1965).

A lively and often controversial 'chronicle of the new drama' selected from the pages of the magazine *Encore*, principal and most consistently intelligent supporter of advanced drama during the years 1956–65. This is not to say that *Encore* or its writers approved of anything and everything presented under the banner of 'new drama' – many of the articles and reviews reprinted in the Reader are sharply and pointedly critical. But the criticism, like the praise, always comes from passionate involvement: even at its most quirky and apparently perverse, it makes you think again.

Martin Esslin, *The Theatre of the Absurd* (Eyre & Spottiswoode, 1962; Doubleday, 1961).

The best general introduction to what the most advanced schools of European drama were up to around the time that *Look Back in Anger* first hit the stage and the British 'new drama' was born. Its direct relevance to British drama is slight, though Harold Pinter and N. F. Simpson do figure among the lesser followers of the Absurdists. The book is, though, a valuable corrective to any tendency we may have to regard drama in English too much as a thing by itself, living in a world of its own.

James Gindin, *Postwar British Fiction* (University of California Press, 1963).

A sane and balanced account of 'new accents and attitudes' in British writing since the end of the war. It includes some mention of the drama, but is valuable especially for filling in the background of the 'angry young men' in literature, by no means all of it angry, during the first post-war decade. The book also gains from being by an American and representing the views of a knowledgeable but disinterested outsider.

John Mander, *The Writer and Commitment* (Secker & Warburg, 1961).

A sustained and largely successful attempt to come to terms with a vague but much cited concept of the late 1950s – that of 'commitment' in art. The author considers various definitions of the term in relation to the writings of those who practise, or claim to practise, it – as well as a number of other writers to whose work the concept seems relevant. The book is particularly helpful in the way it relates the work and ideas of left-wing 'angries' of the 1950s to those of Socialist intellectuals of the 1930s.

John Russell Taylor, *Anger and After* (Penguin Books, 1963).

'A guide to the new British drama' in general, including critical essays on some twenty of the leading dramatists to emerge since 1956 and shorter notes on most of the rest, along with background information on theatres, companies, economic conditions of the British theatre and so on.

J. C. Trewin, *Dramatists of Today* (Staples Press, 1953).

A comprehensive summary, by one of the more conservative British drama critics, of the situation in the British theatre on the eve (as it turned out) of the advent of the 'new drama'. Long and reasonable, if, it now seems to us, much too kindly, studies of the dramatists who were then most approved of by critics and public: Christopher Fry, Terence Rattigan, R. C. Sherriff, Emlyn Williams, etc. At once a warning against over-enthusiasm for the merely new, an invitation to revalue and a vivid picture of everything in the theatre which the 'new drama' felt it most necessary to react violently against.

Kenneth Tynan, *Curtains* (Longmans, 1961; Athenaeum, 1961).

A collection of writings on the theatre and theatrical reviews by one of the leading British critics of the younger generation. Tynan, of course, was the man who most enthusiastically welcomed *Look Back in Anger* at its first appearance on the British stage. His writing on the theatre in general is sometimes passionate, sometimes dutiful, sometimes divided against itself, sometimes stunningly concentrated and to the point. At any rate, it is not often dull, and from reading it *en masse* one gets a remarkably complete picture of what theatre, advanced and reactionary, good, bad and indifferent, was like between 1950 and 1960.

NOTES ON CONTRIBUTORS

GEOFFREY CARNALL is Reader in English Literature at Edinburgh University. Previously he spent some time in India, studying the life and ideas of Gandhi.

HAROLD CLURMAN (1901-80) founded, with Lee Strasberg and Clifford Odets, of the pre-war New York Group Theatre, the history of which he has written in *The Fervent Years*, and more recently he has directed many important productions in London and New York. He was for some years drama critic of *The Nation*, his collected reviews having been published as *Lies Like Truth*.

MARY McCARTHY is a leading American novelist, her best-known books being *The Company She Keeps*, *A Charmed Life* and *The Group*. She has written on theatre sporadically, in *The Partisan Review* and elsewhere, since 1937.

JOHN MANDER (1932–78), poet, critic and political writer. He worked as a journalist in Berlin and London, and was assistant literary editor of the *New Statesman*, and subsequently assistant editor of *Encounter*. He translated several plays from the German, and his other publications include *The Eagle and the Bear*, a study of Berlin (1959), *The Writer and Commitment* (1961), *Berlin: Hostage for the West* (1962), *Great Britain or Little England?* (1963), *Static Society: The Paradox of Latin America* (1969) and *Our German Cousins* (1974).

CHARLES MAROWITZ has been co-editor of the British theatre-magazine *Encore* and of two volumes of essays on theatre, *The Encore Reader* and *Theatre at Work*; he is author of *The Method as Means*, and is a successful director on the London stage.

EDWIN MORGAN is Titular Professor in English Language and Literature at Glasgow University; his books include a translation of Beowulf into modern English verse and a long poem, *Cape of Good Hope*.

GEORGE E. WELLWARTH has been a professional actor in New York and Chicago, has translated a number of French *avant-garde* plays, and was in 1970 appointed Professor of Theatre and Comparative Literature, State University of New York at Binghampton.

KATHERINE J. WORTH is Professor of Drama and Theatre Studies at Royal Holloway College, University of London. Her publications include *The Irish Drama of Europe from Yeats to Beckett* and *Beckett the Shape Changer*.

INDEX